CW00403107

SCOTTIS

Editor
DAVID DAICHES

JOHN GALT

by P. H. Scott

Annals of the Parish, The Ayrshire Legatees, and *The Provost* have been steady favourites of readers since they were first published. It is less well known that John Galt was a novelist of great range, versatility and originality. Two of his longer novels, *The Entail* and *Ringan Gilhaize,* are works of exceptional power. *The Member* was one of the first, and is still one of the most penetrating, political novels. In *Lawrie Todd* and *Bogle Corbet,* he turned his gift for sociological analysis to the early days of the United States and Canada. P. H. Scott, whose previous book, *Walter Scott and Scotland* (Blackwood's 1981), dealt with Galt's contemporary, now explores the range of a novelist whose output and achievement were no less remarkable.

JOHN GALT

P. H. SCOTT

SCOTTISH ACADEMIC PRESS

EDINBURGH

Published by
Scottish Academic Press Ltd.
33 Montgomery Street, Edinburgh EH7 5JX

First published 1985
SBN 7073 0364 8

© 1985 Text and Bibliography
P. H. Scott

Printed in Great Britain by
Clark Constable,
Edinburgh, London, Melbourne

CONTENTS

ABBREVIATED TITLES USED IN REFERENCES

I. JOHN GALT

Autobiography

Aut.   *Autobiography* (2 vols; 1833)
L.L.   *Literary Life and Miscellanies* (3 vols; 1834)

Novels

A.L.   *The Ayrshire Legatees* (1820)
An.   *Annals of the Parish* (1821)
A.W.   *Sir Andrew Wylie of that Ilk* (3 vols; 1822)
B.C.   *Bogle Corbet* (1831)—(References to Vol. I and II are to 1st edition; those to Vol. III to New Canadian Library Edition of 1977.)
Ent.   *The Entail* (1922)
Gath.   *The Gathering of the West* (1822)—(Page references to edition of 1939.)
Las.   *The Last of the Lairds* (1826)—(Page references to edition of 1977.)
L.T.   *Lawrie Todd* (1830)
Mem.   *The Member* (1832)—(Page references to edition of 1975.)
Pro.   *The Provost* (1822)
Rad.   *The Radical* (1832)
R.G.   *Ringan Gilhaize* (1823)
Sb.   *The Steamboat* (1821)—(Page references to edition of 1822.)

II. OTHERS

Ferguson—Adam Ferguson: *An Essay on the History of Civil Society* (1762)—(Ed. of 1978)
Gordon—Ian A. Gordon: *John Galt: The Life of a Writer* (1972)
Jeffrey—Francis Jeffrey: *Contributions to the Edinburgh Review* (1844)—3 vols.
Oliphant—Margaret Oliphant: *Annals of a Publishing House; William Blackwood and His Sons* (1847)—3 vols.

CHAPTER I

INTRODUCTION

In *The House with the Green Shutters*, George Douglas Brown suggests that John Galt is the archetype of a particular kind of Scotsman. "To him there is a railway through the desert where no railway exists, and mills along the quiet stream. And his *perfervidum ingenium* is quick to attempt the realising of his dreams. That is why he makes the best of colonists. Galt is his type."[1] V. S. Pritchett too was struck by this side of Galt's character:

> When one looks at the long list of plays, poems, hack biographies, pamphlets and novels which he wrote, it is a surprise to discover that the main business of his life was buying and selling, pushing plans for colonisation, or for damming great rivers like the Clyde and the St Lawrence, getting canal bills through Parliament and founding towns in Canada. The now thriving town of Guelph in Ontario, was founded by him; he chose its site and planned its institutions; one other town in the same province bears his name.[2]

It may seem strange to speak of a novelist and a professional man of letters in these terms, but Galt was a man of diverse aspirations. Brown may think of him as a peculiarly Scottish type, but the man he most resembles in many ways is Daniel Defoe. Both were Presbyterian. Both were fired with commercial ambitions and wrote about them with enthusiasm; but all the commercial ventures of both ended in failure. Both performed useful, if unorthodox, services for Whitehall, Defoe as a propagandist

and spy to help to push through the Anglo-Scottish
Parliamentary Union of 1707, Galt as an organiser of the
settlement of Ontario. Both were treated shabbily by their
ungrateful employers. Both spent some time in prison,
Defoe for sedition and Galt for debt. But among all these
points of resemblance, the most striking is in their writing.
Both wrote on a great variety of subjects, prose and verse,
books and contributions to periodicals, ranging from hack
work to work of genius, but the best work of both is in a
particular kind of novel. That is, novels usually written in
the first person by an imaginary narrator, which are so
circumstantial and convincing that they can easily be
mistaken for genuine accounts of real events.

If the resemblances between Galt and the 17th-century
Englishman, Daniel Defoe, are fortuitous and paradoxical,
there are more tangible affinities between Galt and his
Scottish contemporary, Walter Scott. There is a curious
similarity in the first place between the early vicissitudes of
Scott's first novel *Waverley* and of the first novel which Galt
began, although not the first to be published, *Annals of the
Parish*. The story about the origins of *Waverley* is well
known. Scott began it in 1805 but abandoned the attempt
after the first few chapters when a friend thought it dull. He
came across the manuscript again in 1813, completed it
and published it with resounding success in 1814. Galt tells
us that he started to write the *Annals* in 1813, but did not
continue because Constable told him that Scottish novels
"would not do".[3] In 1821, after Scott had abundantly
proved that Constable was wrong, Blackwood finally
encouraged Galt to finish the *Annals* by accepting *The
Ayrshire Legatees* for his magazine.

Waverley and the *Annals* have more in common than this
coincidence of dates and publishing history. In his
Memorials, Lord Cockburn describes the reaction in
Edinburgh to the first appearance of *Waverley*: "The
unexpected newness of the thing, the profusion of original
characters, the Scotch language, Scotch scenery, Scotch

men and women, the simplicity of the writing, and the graphic force of the descriptions, all struck us with an electric shock of delight."[4] Much the same might have been said of Galt's Scottish novels, even if Scott's were the first to reach print. Before Scott and Galt, novels set wholly or mainly in Scotland and using the rhythms and vocabulary of Scottish speech were virtually unknown, although there was a strong tradition of oral folk tales. Smollett had sent the Bramble family north of the Border in *Humphry Clinker*, and Scottish characters and Scottish attitudes, but not speech, abound in his other novels. Elisabeth Hamilton's *Cottagers of Glenburnie* (1808) had introduced Scottish speech into a Scottish situation, but it was a dull, moralising work. In more than one respect, Scott and Galt were breaking new ground. With Ramsay, Fergusson and Burns, there had been a great revival of the use of Scots for verse in the 18th century. A similar revival in the use of prose had now found expression in the novel.

Galt's use of Scots was even more extensive than Scott's. With the magnificent exception of *Wandering Willie's Tale*, Scott confined Scots to the conversations of his characters. With his imaginary narrator telling the story in the first person, as in the *Annals* and elsewhere, Galt uses a form of English that is heavily inflected with Scots idiom and vocabulary. A Scottish minister in the 18th century would probably have written a studied, Latinate English prose. Galt's Mr Balwidder writes as he would have spoken. He is almost certainly the model for the very similar type of Scots English which Stevenson used in *Kidnapped* and his other novels set in 18th-century Scotland.

Galt was a deliberate artist in the use of Scots and a life-long enthusiast for its richness and vitality. He made the case for it in one of his first published works, a biographical sketch of John Wilson (1803). In using English, he says, a Scotsman "uses a species of translation, which checks the versatility of fancy, and restrains the genuine and spontaneous flow of his conceptions". It is "the common language of his country, in which he expresses himself with most ease and vivacity".[5] Towards the end of his life, in a note prefixed to his story *The Seamstress* (1833), Galt returned to the subject, referring to "the fortunate circumstances of the Scotch possessing the whole range of the English language, as well as their own, by which they enjoy an uncommonly rich vocabulary".[6] At various times in his writing career, Galt was in the habit of returning to Greenock to refresh his own vocabulary at its source. The occasional Scots word appears in his prose even when he is writing about subjects which have no Scottish connection at all.

The use of Scots by both novelists was not a fortuitous ornament but a necessary consequence of an attempt to record Scottish life before or during a period of rapid change. In the last chapter of *Waverley*, Scott said, "There is no European nation which, within the course of half a century, or little more, has undergone so complete a change as this kingdom of Scotland". He described his objective as "the task of tracing the evanescent manners of his own country". The whole passage, and there are scores of other examples in Scott's writing, is charged both with mixed feelings and emotional involvement. With one part of his mind he accepted, even approved of, "progress"; with another, he resented and regretted many of its consequences, and in particular, the erosion of the Scottish identity. Galt, in spite of his entrepreneurial instincts, responded emotionally in very much the same way. In his *Autobiography*, he describes the experience which gave him the impulse to write the *Annals of the Parish*:

> One Sunday, happening to take a solitary walk to the neighbouring village of Inverkip, I observed that from the time I had been there before, some progress had been made in turning it inside out. The alteration was undoubtedly a great improvement, but the place seemed to me neither so picturesque nor primitive as

the old town, and I could not refrain from lamenting
the change, as one sighs over the grave of an old man.[7]

With both Galt and Scott, it was the fact that they
"could not refrain from lamenting the change" that drove
them to preserve what they could in their Scottish novels.
The Scots language itself was not the least of the values that
was suffering erosion, as Galt was to illustrate quite
deliberately in *The Entail*.

Both Scott and Galt were born in the 1770s and
therefore at the height of that great upsurge of intellectual
energy which we know as the Scottish Enlightenment.
Inevitably, although criticism has been slow to recognise
it, both were heavily influenced by its ideas, aspirations
and methods. There is a passage in Scott's autobiographical memoir which implies that he saw his novels as
illustrating the "general principles" of the "philosophy of
history".[8] This is language which is pregnant with
implications of Enlightenment thought. In the last thirty
years or so, critics of Scott have followed this hint and
found real substance in it, to the point where David
Daiches can say that it is only in the last few years that we
have begun to understand what the novels are really
about.[9] Earlier generations of readers can perhaps be
forgiven for this lack of perception because they were
distracted by the fashionable veneer of the romantic and
picturesque. It was only in his occasional political
pamphleteering that Scott made his debt to Enlightenment philosophy, and in particular to Adam Ferguson,
patent and inescapable.[10]

It was otherwise with Galt. In some of his less successful
books, such as *Rothelan* and *The Spaewife*, he aspired to
historical novels of the Scott type, but his distinctive
manner is something quite different. He argued himself
that they should not be regarded as novels at all but as
"theoretical histories".[11] Here he is using a term which
Dugald Stewart claimed to have introduced for a

particular class of writing much practised by the philosophers of the Scottish Enlightenment. I shall argue that
Galt used the phrase in quite a different sense, even if his
use of it at all reveals a consciousness of Enlightenment
influence. *Annals of the Parish* is the most comprehensive of
his "theoretical histories". It has achieved the unusual
distinction of being described by a historian, G. M.
Trevelyan, as "the most intimate and human picture of
Scotland during her period of change in the reign of
George III".[12] As this suggests, the book is an accurate
reflection of the social atmosphere in a period of rapid
transition, but it also embodies the ideas of the Enlightenment philosophers on the mechanism, nature and effects of
the process of social change. In it Enlightenment ideas
cease to be theoretical abstractions and are given not only
a local habitation and a name but all the reality of human
life. This is done with such skill that it is not obtrusive. The
book can be read purely as a gently ironic comedy of
country life.

In his own comments on his work, Galt insisted that he
had a serious purpose. "I have, in all my works, kept the
instructive principle more or less in view", he wrote in his
Autobiography, and he continued:

> I only desire it to be remembered by my readers that,
> I had an object in view beyond what was apparent. I
> considered the novel as a vehicle of instruction, or
> philosophy teaching by examples, parables, in which
> the moral was more valuable than the incident were
> impressive. Indeed it is not in this age that a man of
> ordinary common sense would enter into competition
> in recreative stories, with a great genius who possessed
> the attention of all. I mean Sir Walter Scott.[13]

When he wrote this, Galt was exaggerating, or perhaps
betraying a twinge of Presbyterian conscience over the
frivolity of writing novels for pleasure alone. There is
generally a vast difference between him and Scott in style

and subject, although there are characters and scenes in both that have a strong affinity. (Bailie Nichol Jarvie would recognise Provost Pawkie as a familiar acquaintance.) Galt was no match for Scott in the "Impressive incidents", or in other words, in the romantic and picturesque. When he attempted such flights as those, he invariably failed, either in some of his unsuccessful novels as a whole or in episodes dragged incongruously into others, much to their detriment. But, of course, that is not the only way in which a novel can be "recreative" or we would now say entertaining. Galt was at his best in the domestic scenes of everyday life, in the shrewd observation of character, in ironic self-revelation, in pungent dialogue in Scots. In all of this, he was continuously entertaining, usually comic, but with a balanced view of life that was not afraid of pathos. Although they are so far apart in their different national traditions and social atmosphere, there is something in Galt's irony, humour and detachment that has similarities with Jane Austen.

Galt enlarged the scope of the novel as a literary form in more than one direction. As he modestly said himself, "I do not think that I have had numerous precursors, in what I would call my theoretical histories of society".[14] He does not give us a list of the books which he included in this category, but there is a recognisable group to which Galt wanted to give the general title of "Tales of the West": *The Ayrshire Legatees, Annals of the Parish, Sir Andrew Wylie, The Provost, The Steam-Boat, The Entail, The Gathering of the West* and *The Last of the Lairds*, as well as a number of short stories. The action of much of *The Ayrshire Legatees* and *Sir Andrew Wylie* is in England, but they begin and end in the West of Scotland. It is there that the others are firmly rooted and in Galt's own life-time or a generation or two before, that is from about 1760 to about 1820. Together, they amount to a comprehensive picture of society in that particular time and place. Of the *Annals* itself, Lionel Stevenson said that it was the first novel in the language that "takes a whole community as its subject".[15] The feeling of community is even stronger if all the novels are taken together because they are full of inter-related cross references so that each complements the others. As Ian Gordon says, they formed the first *roman fleuve*.[16]

Galt especially claimed originality for a novel of rather a different kind, *Ringan Gilhaize*, which he described as "unique".[17] In method, this was not unlike *Annals* or *The Provost* since it was told in the first person by a fictitious narrator. The difference lies first of all in a much wider expanse of time, covering some 150 years by the device of narrator recounting his grandfather's reminiscences as well as his own experiences. Secondly, by making the narrator a Covenanter driven by persecution to fanaticism and the verge of madness, Galt imposed on himself a much more ambitious experiment in historical imagination. His narrator was not only further removed from himself in time than those of the "Tales of the West", but still further in experience, attitude and belief.

Galt was an innovator also of the political novel. *The Provost* was mainly concerned with manipulation on the restricted stage of small-town politics. *Sir Andrew Wylie of that Ilk* moves into the corridors of power in Westminster, and introduces the mechanism of politics as a theme. As Ian Gordon says of this: "Galt ... is a pioneer. While Disraeli and Trollope were still schoolboys, he was quietly initiating the political novel."[18] He went on to write two essentially political novels, *The Member* and *The Radical*. "It makes you wonder", remarks Jo Grimond, "why no one else has done the same thing before or since, not even Disraeli or Trollope."[19] In one of the interwoven plots of the same novel, *Sir Andrew Wylie*, Galt introduces a sub-plot of murder and detection, then still something of an innovation. Reflecting his own experience, Galt was also early on the scene with novels of North American life with *Lawrie Todd* set in the United States and *Bogle Corbet* in Canada. The editor of a recent Canadian edition of the second of these describes it as "the first major work to define Canadianism by reference to an American alternative".[20]

In the pages which follow, I propose to concentrate on these thirteen novels. Galt wrote a great deal more than this, plays, poetry, travel books, biography, miscellaneous journalism as well as other novels. Much of this miscellaneous writing is by no means without interest, especially his *Life of Byron* and his *Autobiography*, but little of it approaches the originality, vitality and humour of the thirteen novels. It is on these that Galt's claim to be regarded as an important writer must rest. By themselves they are a substantial achievement. Some of them have seldom been out of print since they were first published over 150 years ago; others have been largely neglected and have only recently been rediscovered. In his own time, Galt was esteemed by Scott, Byron, Jeffrey and Coleridge. For the mid-19th century, much of Galt's work was too realistic and outspoken for the genteel sensibilities of the age, but since about 1890 appreciation of him has been widening and deepening.

Galt has a penetrating grasp of character and human motives, an exuberant sense of comedy and a delicate irony. He neither shrinks from pathos nor wallows in it. He faces up to the problems of his own time with realism and intelligence. His work was much influenced by Scottish Enlightenment thought and is itself one of the achievements of that remarkable period. Few novelists have been so aware of political and economic realities. In technique, his novels are varied and inventive. Very often his ideas were in advance of his time and now strike us as surprisingly modern. Of *Ringan Gilhaize* which was less successful than he hoped, Galt wrote in his *Literary Life*: "Whatever may be the blindness of the present age, thank God there will be a posterity".[21] His confidence was not misplaced.

REFERENCES

1. George Douglas Brown: *The House with the Green Shutters*, Chap. XI.
2. V. S. Pritchett: *The Living Novel* (1946), p. 38. The Town of Galt has now, unaccountably, been re-named Cambridge.
3. Aut., Vol. II, pp. 227–8.
4. Henry Cockburn: *Memorials of His Time* (Ed. of 1872), p. 241.
5. Prefixed to John Leyden's edition of *Scotish* (sic) *Descriptive Poems* (1803), p. 14.
6. John Galt: Note to "The Seamstress". Ian Gordon's edition of *Selected Short Stories*, p. 21.
7. Aut., Vol. II, p. 227.
8. Sir Walter Scott: *Autobiography* (printed as Chapter I of J. G. Lockhart's *Memoirs of Sir Walter Scott*, ed. of 1900), Vol. I, p. 29.
9. David Daiches—In a lecture at a Saltire Society Conference in St Andrews, September 1975.
10. See on this point my paper on "The Politics of Sir Walter Scott" in *Scott and His Influence*, edited by H. H. Alexander and David Hewitt (1983), pp. 208–19.
11. Aut., Vol. II, p. 219.
12. G. M. Trevelyan: *English Social History* (ed. of 1945), p. 456.
13. Aut., Vol. II, p. 210.
14. Aut., Vol. II, p. 220.
15. Lionel Stevenson: *The English Novel* (1960), p. 217.
16. Gordon, p. 41.
17. Aut., Vol. II, p. 220.
18. Gordon, p. 47.
19. Jo Grimond: *The Sunday Times*—24 August 1975, p. 26.
20. Elisabeth Waterson: Introduction to New Canadian Library edition of Bogle Corbet (Vol. III)—1977—p. 2.
21. L.L., Vol. I, p. 258.

CHAPTER II

LIFE

John Galt was born on the 2 May 1779, in Irvine, a seaport on the coast of Ayrshire. His father was a sea-captain and the owner of his own ship engaged in the trade with the West Indies. When John was 10, the family moved the thirty miles or so to Greenock, on the Clyde estuary. The first 25 years of Galt's life were spent in this western corner of Scotland between these two places. It was the part of the world in which he afterwards set his "Tales of the West". Irvine was the original of the Gude-town of *The Provost* and Dreghorn, a village two miles to the east, of the Dalmailing of *Annals of the Parish*. As he said in his *Autobiography*, he had a "vivid recollection of many things"[1] in these early years which he afterwards introduced in his novels. This process of absorption was helped rather than hindered by the fact that he was, in his own words, a "soft, ailing and growing boy"[2] who was never in perfect health. This kept him from the ordinary ploys of boys of his age and interfered with his education, but it encouraged him to spend much of his time listening to the tales of the old women of the neighbourhood. He describes this in his *Autobiography* and attributes the same habit to Andrew Wylie in the early chapters of the novel. "He was also distinguished from all the lads of his own age, for the preference which he gave to the knacky conversation of old and original characters."[3] He was filling his head with the current Scots speech of an older generation and it is no accident that old women are among the most vivid characters in his novels.

His poor health as a child also, as with Walter Scott, disposed him to books. He had, he tells us, a "passion for reading".[4] This was resisted, happily without success, by his mother who evidently felt that this was not the best way for a growing boy to spend his time. In spite of this disagreement, this relationship was close, and she contributed to the stock of language, character and incident which Galt was unconsciously storing in his head. He tells us that she was "very singular . . . with great natural humour and a keen perception of the ridiculous",[5] and with a taste for the striking use of language. She was the original, Galt says in his *Autobiography*, of Mrs Pringle in *The Ayrshire Legatees* "and was recognised by herself with some surprise and good humour".[6] His father, described by Galt as a man "of an easy nature",[7] seems to have had little influence on him. Perhaps he was away at sea for much of the time.

In the 14 or 15 years which he spent in Greenock Galt was able to indulge his taste for books by joining a subscription library founded in 1783.[8] It was, he says, "a selection of books formed with uncommon judgement and taste. The useful predominates in the collection and to this circumstance, probably, should be attributed my habitual partiality for works of a solid character."[9] Indeed, the catalogue of the time includes all the standard works of the Scottish Enlightenment — Robertson, Hume, Smith, Ferguson, Reid, Beattie and the *Statistical Account* — as well as Malthus, Bentham, Godwin, Burke, Condercet, Voltaire, Rousseau, Montesquieu and Franklin.[10] On one notable occasion at least, Galt intervened actively, in the conduct of the Library. When the fear of revolutionary ideas from France was at its height, the Librarian purged dangerous books, such as those of Holcraft and Godwin, from the shelves. Galt successfully led the opposition and was able not only to have the books restored but to have the subscription raised to buy more of the same kind. This was in spite of the fact that he always regarded himself as a Tory, even if one of an unusually irreverent and egalitarian kind. Indeed his Toryism was something of a paradox. As he said in his *Literary Life*: "I was surely born a Radical, and owe my Tory predilections entirely to a prankful elf, ... delighting in the ridiculous ...".[11] "My best friends have been whigs, and the tories I have always thought by far too intractable."[12]

The Greenock Subscription Library was in effect Galt's university and, from the evidence of his writing, it seems to have given him a good grounding in Scottish Enlightenment thought. He also (like Burns and Scott) indulged in the good old Scottish practice of joining in a society for debate and intellectual exercise. He began, with his friends William Spence and James Park, to hold monthly meetings where they read essays to one another "about every sort of subject".[13] It was not long before they aspired to print. Galt's first success was in 1803 when John Leyden printed his essay on John Wilson as an introduction to his edition of *Scotish* (sic) *Descriptive Poems*. About the same time, Galt appeared too in the *Scots Magazine* with extracts from his *The Battle of Largs: A Gothic Poem*, and a translation of an Ode of Horace in Scots. He wrote a tragedy about Mary Queen of Scots. Throughout his life, Galt continued to write verse, but it is not his natural element. His verse is flat, conventional and, to modern taste at least, frankly unreadable. As Galt himself remarks,[14] it is a curious coincidence that he should have begun to write narrative poems on themes of Scottish history at about the same time as Walter Scott. (The *Lay of the Last Minstrel* was published in 1805.) In Galt's case, it was a false start.

One of the activities of this literary society in Greenock gives us our first glimpse of Galt through the eyes of a contemporary, and that no less than James Hogg. Early in 1804, Galt and his friends invited Hogg to a dinner in his honour. This is his description of the evening and of Galt in particular:

> The first thing that drew my attention to him was an argument about the moral tendency of some of

Shakespeare's plays, in which, although he had two opponents, and one of them both obstinate and loquacious, he managed his part with such good nature and such strong emphatic reasoning, that my heart whispered to me again and again "This is no common youth". Then his stories of old-fashioned and odd people were so infinitely amusing, that his conversation proved one of the principal charms of that enchanting night. The conversation of that literary community of friends at Greenock as well as their songs and stories, was much above what I had ever been accustomed to hear.[15]

Evidently, Galt was already displaying in conversation some of the qualities which afterwards appeared in his books.

Meanwhile, he had started to earn his living as a junior clerk with merchants in Greenock. He stayed with them from the age of 17 to 25, but then left impetuously after a brush with an abusive client. On an impulse, he decided to seek his fortune in London. This was not the only time in his life that he suddenly changed course in mid-stream without any very obvious reason. His career in Greenock had been going well; he had many friends and a growing reputation. His feelings seem to have been mixed. He said in his *Autobiography* that his fifteen years in Greenock were "a large oasis in the desert of my life, and much of my good nature towards mankind is assuredly owning to my associates there. I have met, no doubt, with many more accomplished, but never with better men."[16] But a page or two later he adds, "I felt at Greenock as if I was never in my proper element".[17] He returned frequently to Greenock throughout his life, and settled there at the end. When he was travelling in the Mediterranean and was struck by the beauty of the scene, it was the resemblance to the prospect of Argyllshire from the hills above Greenock that came irresistibly to his mind.[18] His affection for his native place was the impulse that led him to write a whole series of novels about it; but at the same time he had a restless urge to see other places and conquer new ground. D. M. Moir, who knew him well, said that "the love of distinction was Galt's ruling passion, and perhaps the fault of his life was, that he had not steadily pursued it by one avenue".[19]

He arrived in London in May 1804 armed with a pile of letters of introduction. They did him little good. His account of hawking them around the recipients reminds one inevitably of Wilkie's well-known painting on the subject. This is more than a coincidence because the two men corresponded[20] and there are frequent echoes of Galt's novels in Wilkie's paintings. The affinity between the writer and the painter was noticed by Galt's contemporaries. Byron, for instance, said to Lady Blessington: "The characters in Mr Galt's novels have an identity that reminds me of Wilkie's pictures".[21]

For a time, Galt led a lonely life in the big city in, as he says, "the disconsolate condition of him who has no friend in Babylon".[22] He studied political economy and commercial history and practice. Writing he did not abandon altogether but in a field far removed from Gothic poetry. He began a life of Wolsey. For the *Philosophical Magazine* (edited by another emigré Scot, Alexander Tilloch) he wrote *An Essay on Commercial Policy* and, with more significance for his subsequent development, a *Statistical Account of Upper Canada*. There are two points of interest in this. First of all, it is the first sign of an interest in Canada, which, he tells us, had been implanted in him as a small boy when he saw a print of the Niagara Falls, "an event which has had a singular influence on my life".[23] Also, it shows the influence on his mind of Sir John Sinclair's *Statistical Account of Scotland*, which is part of the background to the *Annals of the Parish*. He could have had no other example in mind because the phrase, and the adjective 'statistical' itself, had been introduced into the language by Sinclair.

Literature, of course, was not his whole life. Indeed,

surprising as it may be in the light of his huge output, Galt professed not to take writing very seriously. "It is a poor trade", he said in his *Autobiography* and "it has been only when I had nothing else to do, that I have had recourse to this secondary pursuit".[24] Scott often said much the same. Perhaps both of them were influenced in this as in much else by Adam Ferguson. In his *Essay on the History of Civil Society*, he had argued against "the false importance which is given to literature, as a business for life".[25] At all events, Galt continued to try to make his way in business. A partnership venture, with capital provided by his father, ended in bankruptcy. He thought that he might make a career at the Bar and entered Lincoln's Inn. This too was abortive. After a few months, he made another of his sudden decisions and set off in 1809 to travel around the Mediterranean.

He spent two years on this journey, financed presumably by his tolerant father. Whether it was his object or not, he broadened his experience and collected material for subsequent books. In Gibraltar he accidentally met Byron, travelled with him to Malta and ran into him again in Athens, as he afterwards recorded in his *Life of Lord Byron* (1830). During the journey, he wrote another Statistical Account; this time of Sicily. He almost acquired the Elgin Marbles, when Lord Elgin's agent was for a time short of funds. Another of his unsuccessful business ventures was an attempt to break the Napoleonic blockade by shipping goods into central Europe through Turkey. On his return, he published his first book, *Travels in the Years, 1809, 1810 and 1811*.

His acquaintance with Byron continued after they both returned to London. This gives us another impression of Galt as he appeared to a contemporary. Byron told Lady Blessington: "I am pleased at finding he is as amiable a man as his recent works prove him to be a clever and intelligent author. When I knew Galt, years ago, I·was not in a frame of mind to form an impartial opinion of him; his mildness and equanimity struck me even then; but, to say the truth, his manner had not deference enough for my then aristocratical taste, and finding I could not awe him into a respect sufficiently profound for my sublime self, either as a peer or an author, I felt a little grudge towards him that has now completely worn off."[26]

In October 1811 Galt returned to London, by way of Greenock. He saw a number of his books through the press, the *Travels*, the *Life of Wolsey* and a collection of blank-verse plays. Again he made some vain attempts to establish himself in commerce. The last of these took him once more to Gibraltar where he spent a year working for a Glasgow merchant. Ill health brought him back to London in 1813. He was 34, miserable, depressed and an apparent failure. With the collapse of all his commercial ambitions, he reconciled himself to the life of a hack writer and settled down to family life by marrying the daughter of his literary patron, Alexander Tilloch. At about the same time, he took on the job of lobbying Parliament on behalf of the Union Canal between Edinburgh and Glasgow. This gave him the familiarity with Westminster and Whitehall which was the basis subsequently of his venture into Canadian affairs and of his political novels.

After all these false starts, and much miscellaneous writing which need not detain us, Galt suddenly found his métier. The idea which became *Annals of the Parish* had been fermenting in his mind for years. By 1813 he was ready to offer it to Constable, but his abrupt rejection of the whole idea of a novel on a Scottish subject made Galt put it aside. Within a year or two the literary climate had been transformed by the explosive success of the Waverley novels, and Galt found an enthusiastic reception from another Edinburgh publisher, William Blackwood. In 1819 Galt had started to submit miscellaneous articles to *Blackwood's Magazine*, but in March 1820 he wrote to offer something very different, *The Ayrshire Legatees*, an account in the form of letters of the visit of an Ayrshire minister and his family to London to collect a legacy. It ran in monthly parts in the magazine from June 1820 to February 1821 and was an immediate success. For the first time in print, Galt was drawing on his observation of the life of the west of Scotland, and of the Scot in London, and giving free play to his comic and vivid imagination, his ironic intelligence and his linguistic resourcefulness in Scots. "I am convinced that is not in character only, but in all things, that an author should have natural models before him", Galt commented in his *Autobiography*.[27] In *The Ayrshire Legatees*, he put this idea into practice for the first time.

For the next three years, the other "Tales of the West" followed at an astonishing pace (another parallel with Walter Scott), either first in monthly parts in *Blackwood's Magazine* or, with the larger works, immediately as books: *The Steamboat*, and *Annals of the Parish* in 1821; *Sir Andrew Wylie*, *The Gathering of the West*, *The Provost* and *The Entail* all in 1822. In that one year, Blackwood's published ten volumes of Galt in seven months. Some of these were quite short, but two, *Sir Andrew Wylie* and *The Entail*, were full-length 3-volume novels. At least three, *Annals*, *The Provost* and *The Entail*, were masterpieces.

In the 163 years of its existence *Blackwood's Edinburgh Magazine*, to use the full title, introduced many important new writers to the public and made a lasting impression on the literary scene on Scotland and beyond. Without it Galt, like many others, might never have found his real métier or his public. He was aware of his debt to William Blackwood, the founder of the magazine and the first of a whole line of the family who controlled both it and the publishing firm. In his *Autobiography*, Galt said of him: 'if there be any originality in my Scottish class of compositions, he is entitled to be considered as the first person who discovered it".[28] But the relationship between the two men was not without its tensions and disadvantages as well as benefits. Blackwood was an experienced and shrewd publisher with his own strong ideas of what the public wanted to read. Galt, at the beginning at least, was an unknown and aspiring author who needed a Scottish publisher. The result was a stream of comment, amendments and proposals from Blackwood which was sometimes helpful but which could also distort Galt's original intention. Galt went to Edinburgh to write *Sir Andrew Wylie* quite literally under Blackwood's roof. Left to himself, he would have written something like the *Annals* or *The Provost*, compact, coherent and to the purpose. Blackwood wanted a best-selling novel, full of plot, diversity and striking incident. The result was a padding out and a diffusion which distracted from the force of Galt's opening and conclusion. "It is, perhaps, much better than what I had intended", Galt wrote in his *Literary Life*, "but I repine at the change I was induced to make on my original, which was the exhibition of the rise and progress of a humble Scotchman in London. The incidents are by far too romantic and uncommon to my own taste and are only redeemed from this extravagance, by the natural portraiture of the characters. ... It is far too much like a common novel, to afford me satisfaction."[29]

Something similar, though less drastic, happened to *The Entail*. He went to Greenock to write it where he was both free from Blackwood's interference and at the well-head of his linguistic source. He did, however, go to Edinburgh when he was still writing the last volume and this too is marred by the intrusion of incongruous, romantic incident. After this, Galt broke for a time with Blackwood and gave his next novel, the remarkable *Ringan Gilhaize*, to another Edinburgh publisher, Oliver and Boyd (1823). For them, Galt wrote another two much less successful historical novels, *The Spaewife* and *Rothelan*. He had followed Scott into the more distant past where he was distinctly not at home.

In spite of all this literary activity, and his critical and popular success, Galt had not abandoned his other

ambitions. His childhood interest in Canada had been kept
alive by news from a cousin who had settled there. He had
years of experience in lobbying Parliament and Government departments. These two strands came together in
December 1820, when he was appointed as the agent for a
group of claimants in Upper Canada. They had suffered
loss when the United States invaded Canada in the War of
1812 and looked to the British Government for compensation. Galt undertook to act on their behalf with
payments by results. Two years uphill work produced a
scheme which the Government, as is their way, finally
evaded. Galt found an alternative. There were vast tracts
of unsettled land in Canada, known as the Clergy and
Crown Reserves. If a Company could be formed to raise
the necessary capital, these territories could be developed
and the land sold to immigrants, with enough profit to
settle the claims. Such a company was formed in July 1824
with Galt as Secretary. Five Commissioners, of whom Galt
was one, went to Canada in 1825 to investigate and report.
Eventually a Charter was granted and the scheme put into
effect with Galt in charge as Supervisor at the substantial
salary of £1,600. In spite of Galt's efforts, the interests of
the claimants were gradually abandoned and the Colonial
Office insisted on retaining the revenue.

Galt sailed for Canada to take up his appointment in
1826. Before he left he had restored relations with
Blackwood and left with his manuscript of *The Last of the
Lairds*, a return to his best manner and the final volume of
the series which had started with the *Annals*. Blackwood, as
usual, was prolific with advice. A few days before he sailed
Galt, with his patience and time running out, wrote to one
of Blackwood's associates to give him a free hand to do
what he liked with the text. This was D. M. Moir, well
known in the pages of *Blackwood's Magazine* as Delta, a
friend of Galt, a neighbour for a time when Galt took a
house at Eskbank near Edinburgh and his first biographer.
He interpreted his editorial freedom liberally, bowdler-

ising and toning down and even adding a new ending.
Fortunately the original has survived and it was published for the first time in 1976.

For just over two years, 1827 to early 1829, Galt threw
his energy into the development of a million acres of
virtually virgin land between Lake Huron and Lake
Ontario. He organised the felling of forests, the building of
roads, bridges and canals, the sale of land to settlers, the
foundation of the towns of Guelph and Goderich. At last,
he had scope to come to grips with practical affairs on a
great scale. He felt, as he wrote in his *Autobiography*, that he
was "entering seriously the arena of my life".[30] His family
came out to join him and he looked forward to years of
solid achievement. It came to an abrupt end. He had fallen
foul of colonial officialdom, for whom, as for Lord Byron,
he was not sufficiently deferential. His Tory radicalism
seemed to them, not unreasonably, more radical than
Tory. Discreet hints, then as now a powerful instrument of
the establishment, reached the ears of his Directors in
London. They were worried about the safety of their
capital and a quick return on it, and alarmed by Galt's
enthusiasm and social conscience. An accountant was sent
out to spy and report. When Galt realised this, he decided
to go to London to argue his own case. Before he took ship
in New York, he learned that the Directors had replaced
him without even the bleak courtesy of formal dismissal.
"Although I myself say it", he afterwards wrote in a letter
to Moir, "it has fallen to the lot of few to have done so
much for any country and to be so used."[31] Galt's fall from
the pinnacle of ambition to abject humiliation could
hardly have been more sudden or complete. He arrived
back in Liverpool on 20 May 1829; by 15 July he was
arrested for debt and he spent the next few months in the
King's Bench Prison.

Once again, after this brief Canadian interlude, Galt
took up his pen to earn his living. He wrote on a wide
variety of economic and other subjects for *Blackwood's*

Magazine as well as a sequence of short stories in Scots. From 1830 onwards, he also became a regular contributor to *Fraser's Magazine*. For a London publisher, Colburn and Bentley, he wrote on commission and under pressure several three-volume novels. In his *Literary Life*, Galt said that he "would not wish to be estimated"[32] by them, but they included his two novels set in North America, *Lawrie Todd* (1830), and *Bogle Corbet* (1831) which are not negligible. They also published his *Life of Lord Byron* (1830) which caused more controversy than any other of Galt's work and went through five editions in two years. Shortly afterwards, Galt escaped from the tyranny of the commissioned three-volume novel, to break into new ground of his own choice, the political novels, *The Member* and *The Radical*. Both were published in 1832, the year of the Parliamentary Reform Act.

In January 1832, Thomas Carlyle met Galt at a dinner party in London and made an entry in his note-book which gives us another contemporary impression:

> Galt looks old, is deafish; has the air of a sedate Greenock Burgher; Mouth indicating shy humour, and self-satisfaction; the eyes old and without lashes, give me a sort of *wae* interest for him. He wears spectacles, and is hard of hearing: a very large man; and eats and drinks with a certain west-country gusto and research. Said little; but that little peaceable, clear and gutmüthig. Wish to see him also again.[33]

Clearly, Galt's health was already failing. According to R. P. Gillies, who knew him, he never, in fact, fully recovered from the effect of his imprisonment.[34] Towards the end of the same year he had a stroke, which left him, for a time, unable to walk or hold a pen. He continued his work by dictation and in this sorry state composed his *Autobiography* (1833). Not surprisingly he was mainly concerned to justify his role in Canada and he said very little about his books or indeed about his private life. A few months later, he produced a new version, the *Literary Life*, which is our main source of information about Galt's own view of his work.

In 1834 Galt returned to Greenock. For a year or two he continued to write short stories[35] in his "Tales of the West" manner with undiminished zest and humour. He had a ready market for them in *Tait's Edinburgh Magazine*. There is something especially appropriate in this, because it was edited by Mrs Christian Johnstone. She had written one of the first perceptive reviews of the *Annals* on their publication in 1821 and had remained an enthusiast for Galt ever since. These stories were his last substantial work. He stayed in Greenock, at the heart of the country of the "Tales of the West", until his death on 11 April 1839.

REFERENCES

1. Aut., Vol. I, p. 3.
2. Aut., Vol. I, p. 9.
3. A.W., Chap. VIII.
4. Aut., Vol. I, p. 17.
5. Aut., Vol. I, p. 16.
6. Aut., Vol. II, p. 229.
7. Aut., Vol. I, p. 16.
8. W. R. Aitken: *A History of the Public Library Movement in Scotland* (1971), p. 21.
9. Aut., Vol. I, p.17.
10. Erik Frykman: *John Galt and 18th Century Scottish Philosophy* (Papers of the Greenock Philosophical Society, 1953), p. 9.
11. L.L., Vol. I, p. 235.
12. Aut., Vol. II, p. 229.
13. Aut., Vol. I, p. 45.
14. Aut., Vol. I, p. 48.
15. James Hogg: *Reminiscences of Some of his Contemporaries*, quoted by Jennie W. Aberdein in *John Galt* (1936), p. 27.
16. Aut., Vol. I, p. 34.
17. Aut., Vol. I, p. 36.
18. Aut., Vol. I, p. 145.
19. D. M. Moir: *Bibliographical Memoir* prefixed to edition (N.D.) of *Annals of the Parish* and *The Ayrshire Legatees*, p. cxi.

20. Gordon, pp. 10 & 11.
21. Countess of Blessington: *Conversations of Lord Byron* (1934), p. 74.
22. Aut., Vol. I, p. 70.
23. Aut., Vol. I, p. 7.
24. Aut., Vol. I, p. 85.
25. Ferguson, p. 31.
26. Blessington: *op. cit.*, p. 249.
27. Aut., Vol. I, p. 135.
28. Aut., Vol. II, p. 235.
29. L.L., Vol. I, p. 244.
30. Aut., Vol. II, p. 1.
31. D. M. Moir: *op. cit.*, p. xcvii.
32. L.L., Vol. I, p. 317.
33. *Two Note Books of Thomas Carlyle*, ed. E. C. Norton (1898), Entry for 21 Jan. 1832.
34. R. P. Gillies: *Memoirs of a Literary Veteran* (3 Vols.; 1851), Vol. 3, p. 60.
35. Gordon: pp. 125–37.

CHAPTER III

ANNALS OF THE PARISH (1821)

I begin with *Annals of the Parish* for more than one reason. In the first place, as we have seen, it was the first novel which Galt started although it was not the first to be finished or published. Secondly, it is to my mind the most sustained, homogeneous and subtle of Galt's particular kind of novel. Galt himself did not agree: "I am led from many circumstances to conclude that this simple work is considered to be best of my productions; but although willing to regard it among the most original, I do not myself think so".[1] Coleridge praised *The Provost* for its quality of "unconscious, perfectly natural Irony of Self-Delusion, in all parts intelligible to the intelligent Reader, without the slightest suspicion on the part of the Autobiographer".[2] He is perfectly right of course; but, it seems to me that this same quality is displayed with much greater complexity and delicacy in the *Annals*. Others, including Scott, Byron or Coleridge again, have singled out *The Entail*. Certainly that is a much more ambitious work with greater psychological range and emotional depth than the *Annals*; but it is not of uniform excellence and has some incongruous episodes, even if they were inserted to please William Blackwood. Galt would probably have given first place to *Ringan Gilhaize*. That too is an ambitious and impressive book, but it has to be considered on its own. It is not representative, as the *Annals* are, of a whole distinctive *genre* of Galt novels.

Galt then described the *Annals* as a "simple work". So in a sense it is, but it is a deceptive simplicity. He did not think that it was a novel at all, because it was "so void of

anything like a plot, that it lacks in the most material
feature of a novel". He goes on to make a different claim for
it. "Fables are often a better way of illustrating truths than
abstract reasoning and it is in this class of compositions I
would place the Annals of the Parish."[3] Evidently, he
intended the apparent simplicity to carry more significance than might appear on the surface.

In form, the book is simple and straightforward enough.
It purports to be "a faithful account"[4] of his ministry by
the Rev. Mr Balwhidder, minister of the Parish of
Dalmailing from 1760 to 1810. There is a chapter for each
year in which he sets down what seems to him important in
his own and his parishioners' life. His vision is limited not
only by the "narrow sphere"[5] of the parish but because of
his intellectual inadequacy. He recognises this at times
himself: "although there might be some abler with the
head than me".[6] In other ways, his complacency remains
unruffled. He does not doubt that he is the appointed
leader of the community, even if he has to be placed against
popular resistance and even if the congregation only too
obviously begin to escape from his grasp. He never
questions the impregnability of the doctrines acquired in
the "Orthodox University of Glasgow, as it was in the time
of my youth".[7] He relies on the monthly *Scots Magazine* for
his news of the world outside the parish.

With such an observer, one might expect a very limited
and incomplete record of the very period when, as Walter
Scott said, Scotland changed more completely than any
other country in Europe. David Craig has indeed argued
as much. "Because the minister is as conservative and
credulous as many of his parishioners, and because
everything is felt through his mentality, all other possible
life is diminished to his kind of understanding."[8] This
overlooks the subtlety of Galt's method. From the very first
sentence of the book, Galt establishes a conspiracy between
himself and the reader. "In the same year, and on the same
day of the same month, that his sacred Majesty King

George, the third of the name, came to his crown and kingdom, I was placed and settled as the minister of Dalmailing." This establishes the tone from the start. Mr Balwhidder evidently has no sense of proportion. He tells us that he had been "obliged by reason of age and the growing infirmities of my recollection to consent to the earnest entreaties of the Session, and to accept of Mr Amos to be my helper". We see that, whatever his qualities of heart and benevolence, he was never very bright and is now in his dotage. We have to make allowances and read more into his words than Mr Balwhidder intends. As John MacQueen says of him: "The very inadequacy of his responses defines the shape of events more penetratingly than investigations apparently more subtle".[9] It is a sustained exercise in the "irony of self-delusion" which Coleridge noted in *The Provost*, of self-delusion and unconscious self-revelation. Through his account, Mr Balwhidder drops hints of events around him which he understands imperfectly. The reader has been conditioned to look for the wider significance.

Mr Balwhidder's character is not static. He mellows and changes in attitudes and habits, reflecting the changes that were going on around him. This is true in small things as well as great. In chapter II, he disperses a group of women indulging secretly in the new vice of tea-drinking. ("But I gave them a sign by a loud host, that Providence sees all, and it skailed the bike"); by the next chapter, tea reaches the manse, and in chapter XX luxury has advanced so far that Mrs Balwhidder buys a silver teapot. He becomes more tolerant. In chapter XII, Lady Macadam's episopacy prevents "sincere communion" between them. In the last chapter he looks forward to the time "when the tiger of papistry shall lie down with the lamb of reformation, and the vultures of prelacy be as harmless as the Presbyterian doves". Except in the Introduction Mr Balwhidder does not show fore-knowledge of what is to come. Each chapter sounds as though it had been written at the end of the year concerned. This contributes to the feeling both of actuality and of gradual change, but it contradicts the pretence of the Introduction that it was all written by Mr Balwhidder at the end of his life. Galt offers a plausible explanation by referring to the common phenomenon that the memory of old men is often better for distant events than for more recent ones. "As I come towards the events of these latter days," Mr Balwhidder writes in chapter L, "I am surprised to find myself not at all so distinct in my recollection of them, as in those of the first of my ministry." Galt makes a virtue, and adds to the illusion of reality, of what might have been a contradiction in his narrative method.

In his *Autobiography*, Galt gives account of how he came to write the *Annals* and what he was attempting to do. "When very young, I wished to write a book that would be for Scotland what the Vicar of Wakefield is for England. . . . The study, however, was not pursued with any particular intensity, the opportunity indeed was wanting, for our town was large and the clergymen in it too urbane to furnish a model." He then goes on, in a passage from which I have already quoted, to say how he was struck by the improvements in the village of Inverkip and to add:

> While looking at the various improvements around, my intention of writing a minister's sedate adventures returned upon me suddenly and I felt something like that glow with which Rousseau conceived his essay on the arts and sciences.[10]

These references to "progress", "Improvement" and Rousseau become clearer when one realises that Galt is evidently thinking of Rousseau's account in the *Confessions* of the excitement with which he wrote his prize essay for the Academy of Dijon. The subject was "Has the progress of the arts and sciences contributed more to the corruption or purification of morals?".[11]

From Goldsmith's *Vicar of Wakefield*, Galt took no more than the idea of writing a novel in the first person about a country clergyman. That is all that it has in common with the *Annals* and otherwise they could not be more different. The subject of the *Annals* is the whole surrounding community as much as Mr Balwhidder himself. Goldsmith's Dr Primrose is concerned only with his own family and those with whom they are involved in the development of the plot, which is heavily dependent on coincidence. In some of his other novels, Galt helped his plot along with similar improbability, but the *Annals* has no plot at all. The only vicissitudes in *The Vicar of Wakefield* are those of the personal affairs of the characters; there is no hint of social, economic or intellectual change. Such changes are the essential stuff of the *Annals*. Galt was concerned with the same theme as Rousseau, although he made of it a circumstantial story, not an essay. In Mr Balwhidder's words, he was "not writing for a vain world, but only to testify to posterity anent the great changes that have happened in my day and generation".[12]

These changes were transforming the whole of Scotland but they are recorded in the *Annals*, not as a wide, general movement, but in the accumulation of small details as they impinge on Mr Balwhidder and his parishioners. In this way, and with Mr Balwhidder not always fully understanding what is going on, we see a society in rapid transformation through agricultural improvement, industrialisation, new roads and the freer movement of people and ideas, the impact of the American War of Independence and the French Revolution. Usually the changes are introduced from outside, as when Mr Coulter from the Lothians introduces new farming methods or when Mr Cayenne comes back from America and builds a cotton mill. Often they seem to happen for trivial reasons, such as the building of a new road because Lord Eaglesham's coach had been couped into the village midden. It is a society increasing in prosperity but that brings its own complications and disadvantages and "decay in the wanted simplicity of our country ways".[13]

As we have seen, Galt's account of life in a village in Ayrshire in the second half of the 18th century conveys the atmosphere with such accuracy that a serious historian can refer to it almost as though it were a primary historical source.[14] He had two real villages in mind, Inverkip and Dreghorn, but he was writing a fictional account that was meant to be typical not actual; in Mr Balwhidder's words, "but type and index to the rest of the world".[15] It is therefore beside the point to scrutinise the *Annals* for precise conformity to historical fact. One historian who has done this finds 'historical flaws . . . in dates and circumstances", but concedes that "Galt was one of Scotland's finest social commentators".[16] He makes a fair point that Galt failed to do justice to the part played by the lairds in agricultural and industrial development in the 18th century. Galt was a professed Tory, but he was hard on the lairds throughout the "Tales of the West", and the decayed family of Breadland in the *Annals* is no exception.

Galt, as far as I can discover, never mentioned the first *Statistical Account of Scotland* as one of his sources for the *Annals*; but it was inescapably relevant to his purpose. We have noted that it was available to him in the Greenock Library, and that he wrote his own "statistical accounts" of Upper Canada and Sicily. In fact, the original *Statistical Account* amounted to a collection of genuine annals from every parish minister in Scotland covering the period of Galt's book. It was an undertaking astonishing in its originality, scope and successful accomplishment, and in itself one of the great achievements of the Scottish Enlightenment. The work began in 1790 when Sir John Sinclair, with the agreement of the General Assembly, sent a questionnaire to every minister in Scotland about the natural, social, economic and spiritual condition of his parish. The replies were published in 20 volumes between 1791 and 1798. There is a very striking similarity between them and the *Annals*. Galt fleshed out the spare accounts in circumstantial detail. He also allowed Mr Balwhidder to write, as he would have spoken, in Scots with biblical and classical overtones. Otherwise the reports in the *Statistical Account* are time and again echoed in Galt's *Annals*, both in fact and in attitude. For instance, Mr Balwhidder's disapproval of tea drinking may strike us as improbable. There is plenty of evidence in the *Statistical Account* that this view was in fact widespread. The Minister of Coldingham, for instance, describes tea as "superfluous and pernicious".[17] Many of the episodes in the *Annals* could have been suggested by points made in the *Account*. The Minister of Inverkip tells us of the alteration of the alignment of the road on the initiative of a local land-owner.[18] The Irvine account remarks: "there are so many sailors widows, left with numerous families, and often in poor circumstances. This is an evil which calls for redress."[19] Galt gives us an example in Mrs Malcolm, the widow of a shipmaster lost at sea, with a family for whom "she had to work sore for their bit and drap".[20] The whole social atmosphere of the *Account* is reflected in the *Annals*. Almost every Minister tells us that his parishioners are sober, frugal, industrious and (in the words of the Irvine report) "social and cheerful, but seldom riotous".[21] That would be a fair description of the poeple of Dalmailing. The 20 volumes of the *Statistical Account* are a substantial confirmation of the essential accuracy of the *Annals*. The point was noted by one of the first reviewers. Mr Christian Johnstone wrote in the *Inverness Courier* of 10 May 1821: "The Statistical Account of Scotland will never be complete, till the faithful annals of this homely and vivacious chronicler are added to the appendix".

Galt's fidelity to the atmosphere of the period, the accumulation of circumstantial detail, the plausibility of the characters, all contributed to a convincing illusion of reality. John Wilson said that the *Annals* was "not a book but a fact". William Blackwood told Galt that his mother "read the book with great delight, and thought Micah an honest and upright minister of the gospel. But, unfortunately, one of my little boys told her it was a novel, and thus it lost is charms, and she was very angry with us for having deceived her."[22] She was not alone in accepting the book as a genuine autobiography of a real minister.

We have already noted that Galt did not regard the *Annals* and his other books of the kind as novels at all, but as something quite different. In the *Autobiography* and *Literary Life*, he used a number of phrases to describe them. Of the *Annals*, he said that it was "a kind of treatise on the history of society in the West of Scotland during the reign of George the Third" and a fable to illustrate philosophical truths.[23] The whole group of these books he describes as "theoretical histories of society, limited though they were required by the subject, necessarily to the events of a circumscribed locality"[24] and as "philosophical sketches".[25] The question, of course, is what did he mean by these phrases which he did not attempt to explain.

It could, I suppose, be suggested that "theoretical history" is not an inappropriate description of the *Annals* in the sense that it was not a history of an actual place, but of an imaginary one which could nevertheless be taken as typical of a whole society. It was "but a type and index to the rest of the world".[26] The events and the characters were fictional, but they were both credible and representative of a whole society in a particular time and place. But this, in varying degrees, might be said of most novels. Galt was likely to have had a clearer distinction in mind, apart from the absence of a plot, in stressing so emphatically that the *Annals* and his other related books were not novels at all. The clues lie in his use of the terms "theoretical history" and "philosophical". Both had acquired special significance in the way in which they were used in Galt's time in relation to the intellectual movement known as the Scottish Enlightenment.

The term "Theoretical or Conjectural History" was

introduced by Dugald Stewart in his *Account of the Life and Writings of Adam Smith* which appeared in the *Transactions* of the Royal Society of Edinburgh in 1793. He described it as a "species of philosophical investigation" which attempted to deduce from "the known principles of human nature" a process of events for which no evidence remained. "In examining the history of mankind, as well as in examining the phenomena of the material world, when we cannot trace the process by which an event *has been* produced by natural causes."[27] He goes on to give examples from the works of Lord Kames, Adam Smith and John Miller, but he might have mentioned many others including Lord Monboddo, and Adam Ferguson. A large part of Scottish Enlightenment writing was of this kind. It attempted to explain the probable evolution of society, or one of its attributes such as language or economic structure, not by analysing evidence but by speculation. The method was one of abstract reasoning and it was concerned more with principles than with concrete facts.

It would seem that we are a world away from the *Annals* which could not be more particular, local and concrete and apparently less concerned with abstractions. Let me give just one example of the contrast in style and content. Dugald Stewart mentions Adam Smith's chapter on the progress of opulence in different nations in Book III of *The Wealth of Nations* as an example of theoretical history. Smith's discussion of the subject is conducted in such terms as these: "It is the surplus produce of the country only, or what is over and above the maintenance of the cultivators, that constitutes the subsistence of the town, which can therefore increase only with the increase of this surplus produce".[28] Mr Balwhidder on a similar point says:

> This stage-coach I thought one of the greatest conveniences that had been established among us; and it enabled Mrs Balwhidder to send a basket of her fresh butter into Glasgow market, by which, in the

spring and fall of the year, she got a great price, for the
Glasgow merchants are fond of excellent eatables, and
the payment was aye ready money—Tam Whirlitt
the driver paying for the one basket when he took up
the other.[29]

Can two books which are so widely different both be
described as "theoretical history"?

The answer, I think, lies in Galt's underlying purpose,
which he suggests by his repeated use of the word
"philosophical". When the writers of the Scottish Enlightenment described history as philosophical, they meant that
it was concerned not merely with the narrative of events
but with the search for general principles and (in the words
of Lord Kames) "a chain of causes and effects".[30] As we
have seen, Walter Scott used the word in this sense. It is
when we consider these general principles that we see a
very close relationship between the *Annals* and the
conclusions reached by the historians and philosophers of
the Scottish Enlightenment. Like Galt they were concerned with the process of social change, its causes and
effects. Galt's description of the *Annals* as "a kind of treatise
on the history of society" is strikingly reminiscent of the
title of one of the key works of the Enlightenment, Adam
Ferguson's *An Essay on the History of Civil Society*, published
in 1767. This is not a coincidence, because the *Annals* in
almost every chapter reflects Ferguson's ideas.

An Essay on the History of Civil Society is one of these books
which throws up a diversity of ideas, often as a brief
epigram which is left unexplored. There are however a
number of strong connecting themes. Ferguson sees man as
an essentially social creature with his happiness dependent
on membership of a community, and fundamentally
benevolent and compassionate. Man is active, restless and
in constant development, both as an individual and as a
species. In this way, society progresses, but this is so
complex a process that no-one can control or predict it.

"Every step and every movement of the multitude, even in what are termed enlightened ages, are made with equal blindness to the future; and nations stumble upon establishments, which are indeed the result of human action, but not the execution of any human design."[31] The division of labour was a condition of progress; but in the commercial society, which was then beginning to evolve, this could be the degradation of the workers to tasks which require no thought or capacity where they become like part of a machine. Commercial society involved the risks of loss of the values of the community and exposure to "sordid habits and mercenary dispositions".[32]

The themes of the *Annals* are the same, although now, as a "fable", no longer on abstraction but a precise, living example. At the beginning of the book, Dalmailing is very much a community of the kind praised by Ferguson. It is, by and large, compassionate and caring. There is an early example when Mr Balwhidder is rejected because he had been imposed by a patron, but one of the ringleaders changes his mind when he sees the minister going sadly from house to house.[33] The parish is gradually transformed socially, economically and intellectually, without anyone planning or foreseeing the consequences of each step. The road system is improved, with all the economic consequences which that has, apparently because Lord Eaglesham is couped into the midden. Industrialisation arrives and with it both advantages and disadvantages. There is greater prosperity and education and ideas spread more quickly. At the same time, the community spirit is weakened and an "unhealthy melancholy"[34] appears among the workers reduced to a mechanical task.

Galt used the term "theoretical history" almost in an opposite sense from Dugald Stewart as far as method was concerned. At the same time, Galt's use of the term was justified because he was concerned with the same theories as the 18th-century theoretical historians and those of Adam Ferguson in particular. From one point of view,

Annals was a "fable" to illustrate the truth of Ferguson's *Essay.*

Ferguson's organic view of society as a complex growth too complicated to be planned or intended by the individual human will was essentially sceptical both about the role of great men in history and about divine intervention. He saw society evolving as what he called the "mighty engine" as a result of innumerable acts and forces of which the consequences could not be foreseen. He gives no place to God in his system. It is not the least ingenious, or least amusing, aspect of Galt's irony in the *Annals* that he demonstrated Ferguson's theories in action through the eyes of a Minister with a simple faith in Providence. From the very first page of his account, Mr Balwhidder is ready to see "the hand of Providence" at every turn. When his wife's cousin is killed by her mutch catching fire, it is divine chastisement.[35] When new agriculture methods are introduced after the burning of Breadland House, it is Providence "which never fails to bring good out of evil".[36] Mr Balwhidder is able to do this without doing violence to the theories because it is only necessary to ascribe to Providence the role which Ferguson gave to the total effect of imponderable events and forces. Galt takes care to make Mr Balwhidder explain why his old-fashioned faith had remained intact. When he stresses the orthodoxy of Glasgow University when he was a student, he implies that his ideas were formed there before the Moderate movement in the Kirk or the ideas of Hume, Smith and Ferguson had transformed the intellectual climate.

Annals of the Parish is a book which can be read in at least three ways: as an evocation of a period, as an illustration of a theory of social change, or quite simply as a highly entertaining comedy. From each of these points of view, the book is homogeneous and consistent. There is no false note and not a surplus page. To make all this work simultaneously with no sign of tension between the objectives, is artistry of a high order, the more so because of its apparent simplicity. This has always been the most popular of Galt's books. He would have made a notable contribution to our literature, even if he had written nothing else.

REFERENCES

1. L.L., Vol. I, p. 155.
2. *Times Literary Supplement* (Letter from A. J. Ashley), 25 September 1930.
3. L.L., Vol. I, pp. 155-6.
4. An., Introduction.
5. An., Chapt. I.
6. An., Chapt. I.
7. An., Introduction.
8. David Craig: *Scottish Literature and the Scottish People* (1961), p. 158.
9. John MacQueen: *Scottish Bicentenary Essays*, edited by Alan Bell (1973), p. 334.
10. Aut., Vol. II, pp. 226-7.
11. J. J. Rousseau: *Confessions*, Everyman's Library edition (1946), Vol. II, p. 3.
12. An., Chapt. L.
13. An., Chapt. XXIX.
14. See above: Chapt. I, fn. 12.
15. An., Chapt. XLV.
16. Christopher A. Whately in *John Galt 1779–1979* (1979), pp. 61-2.
17. *Statistical Account of Scotland*, Vol. XII (1794), p. 55.
18. *Ibid.*, Vol. IX (1973), p. 100.
19. *Ibid.*, Vol. IX (1973), p. 172.
20. An., Chapt. I.
21. *Stat. Acc.*, Vol. IX (1973), p. 176.
22. Oliphant: Vol. I, pp. 451-2.
23. L.L., Vol. I, pp. 155-6.
24. Aut., Vol. II, pp. 219-20.
25. Aut., Vol. II, p. 221.
26. An., Chapt. XLV.
27. Dugald Stewart in *Collected Works*, edited by Sir William Hamilton (1858), Vol. X, p. 34.
28. Adam Smith: *The Wealth of Nations*, Bk. III, Chapt. I (Everyman's Library Edition), Vol. I, p. 237.
29. An., Chapt. XXX.

30. Lord Kames: *Sketches of the History of Man*, Vol. I, p. 185. (Quoted by Keith Costain: "Theoretical History and the Novel: The Scottish Fiction of John Galt" in *English Literary History*, Vol. 43, n. 3 (1976), p. 362.)
31. Ferguson: p. 122.
32. Ferguson: p. 258.
33. An., Chapt. I.
34. An., Chapt. XXXII.
35. An., Chapt. XVIII.
36. An., Chapt. VII.

CHAPTER IV

THE AYRSHIRE LEGATEES (1820) AND OTHER CONTRIBUTIONS TO BLACKWOOD'S MAGAZINE

The group of novels which Galt described as the "Tales of the West" are all set in the corner of Scotland bounded by the River Clyde and its estuary roughly from Irvine to the south and Greenock and Glasgow to the north and east. In time, they span the period from about the middle of the 18th century to the time when they were written in the 1820s. With the exception of *The Last of the Lairds* (1826) they were all first published, and most of them written, in a great spate of activity between 1820 and 1824. The books have a unity of place and time. Of place, the part of Ayrshire and Renfrewshire where Galt spent the first 25 years of his life. Of time, the period covered either by his own experiences or in the reminiscences of the elderly whose conversations he cultivated. He was writing of what he knew either directly or vicariously.

In spite of these unities and the way in which the books are linked by characters straying from one to the other, they are of three different kinds in length and format. At one end of the scale are those written primarily for serial publication in *Blackwood's Magazine*, although afterwards also published as books. They are short, loosely constructed, and often topical, and are admirably adapted to the requirements of the magazine reader. The first to be published, *The Ayrshire Legatees* (Magazine, June 1820 to February 1821 and as a book, 1821) was of this kind. It was followed by *The Steamboat* (Magazine, February to December 1821; book 1822), and *The Gathering of the West*

(Magazine, December 1822). The next group are the short, one-volume novels with a more coherent and rounded structure. *Annals of the Parish* (1821) was the first of these, and the others are *The Provost* (1822) and *The Last of the Lairds* (1826). In these books, Galt was not working to imposed constraints either of brevity or length and he was therefore able to develop the central idea fully and homogeneously. At the other end of the scale are the full-length three-volume novels, the format which was fashionable at the time. These are *Sir Andrew Wylie* (January 1822) and *The Entail* (December 1822). This more diffuse form did not suit Galt; he was inclined to meet the demands of the three volumes by padding out the book with extraneous material. It was only in *Ringan Gilhaize*, a book of a different kind, that he was able to maintain homogeneous treatment at such length.

The Ayrshire Legatees (1820)

The Ayrshire Legatees owes an obvious debt to Smollett's *Humphry Clinker* (1771), which is an account of the travels through England to Scotland and back of Matthew Bramble with his sister, nephew and niece, told by means of their letters. Galt sends his Rev. Zachariah Pringle to London to collect a legacy along with his wife, son and daughter and similarly they each give their account of their experiences in letters. There are similarities between the characters of the two books. Tabitha Bramble's malapropisms and eccentric spelling, for example, are matched by Mrs Pringle's, and there are clear affinities between the young nephew and niece is one book and the son and daughter in the other. There are parallels too in the underlying themes of the two books. Both were concerned with social and economic change in Scotland. Smollett did this explicitly as in the discussion between Bramble and Lismahago on the effects of the Anglo-Scottish Union of 1707.[1] Galt preferred to leave the reader to draw his own conclusions from hints and implications.

Galt also added a new dimension to the epistolatory technique by a simple device. All the letters from the Pringle family are addressed to their various friends left behind in Dr Pringle's parish in Garnock, "pleasantly situated between Irvine and Kilwinning", and therefore not far from the Dalmailing of the *Annals*. It is the habit of the recipients to read them to their friends and Galt supplements the letters by short passages of narrative to record their reactions.

> Just as Mr Snodgrass concluded the last sentence, one of the Clyde skippers, who had fallen asleep, gave such an extravagant snore, followed by a groan, that it set the whole company a-laughing, and interrupted the critical strictures which would otherwise have been made on Mr Andrew Pringle's epistle. "Damn it," said he, "I thought myself in a fog, and could not tell whether the land ahead was Plada or the Lady Isle". Some of the company thought the observation not inapplicable to what they had been hearing.[2]

By this device, Galt achieves several purposes simultaneously. Part of his purpose in the book was to show the differences in social behaviour and attitudes between the small village community and the town, Edinburgh and, in particular, London. He shows the village functioning as a community with its intimacies and its own standards of values. He counterpoints the reactions of the Pringle family to their experiences in the world outside by the responses of the recipients of the letters. Also we are not left entirely alone to form our judgement of the various members of the Pringle family; their pretensions and failings are brought home by the shrewd responses of the people of Garnock.

The contrasts are not only between town and country but between generations. Dr Pringle is a Presbyterian minister of views as orthodox as Mr Balwhidder himself. He is on his guard against the "relics of popery". For him, "the Church of England is not so well informed and purged as ours from the abominations of the leaven of idolatry".[3] Galt gives us a hint that, like Mr Balwhidder, he has not been able to adapt sufficiently to hold the attention of the new men, the weavers, who have joined his parish. He is ready to retire with his inherited fortune, but not to leave Scotland or his familiar Ayrshire. His son is another matter. He has been called to the Bar in Edinburgh and exposed, though a Tory, to the new influences. "I have had my doubts", his father admits, "that Andrew Pringle's principles have not been strengthened by the reading of the *Edinburgh Review*."[4] Like his sister, he happily adjusts to his new fortune and the temptations of London. The fortune of the Pringle family become a symbol of the pressures of Anglicisation which were in the early 19th century beginning to bear heavily on the new generation. It was a pressure which Galt himself had felt.

In his *Autobiography*, Galt said that Andrew Pringle was "represented as a tory Scottish advocate of the ultra class, and, as such, imbued with antipathies that have their origin in political opinions: under a show of candour he has strong prejudices".[5] He goes on to deny that he was in any sense a self-portrait or that his letters reflected Galt's opinions, as some readers had apparently supposed. In fact, as we have seen in the remark of the Clyde skipper, Galt's portrait of Andrew is by no means sympathetic. Like his sister, although with more pretension, he is shown as silly, shallow and selfish. Galt's feelings are evidently on the side of the older generation whose heads are not turned by their sudden fortune but stay true to the traditional values of their own commuity.

The Ayrshire Legatees is not an extended study like the *Annals* in the evolution of a society over a lifetime and it is narrower in its range of interests as well as in time. It is an episode, although one full of illuminating details. Galt often makes his points in an aside of a sentence or two. We see that a new spirit has entered the Kirk where Mr

Snodgrass, who stands in for Dr Pringle and eventually replaces him, is discovered to be reading *Ivanhoe* on a Sunday morning.[6] We see the change in the attitude of the generations when the old men on Dr Pringle's return "stood up and reverently took off their hats and bonnets", but "the weaver lads gazed with a melancholy smile".[7]

It is not surprising that among Galt's novels *The Ayrshire Legatees* has been second only to the *Annals* in steady popularity. The letter form enabled Galt to display his ability to make his characters reveal more than they supposed through four different personalities. The serious overtones of the book are deliciously concealed below a comedy of gentle mockery. It is full of good jokes. Although each of the magazine instalments could be read in isolation, the book as a whole has a shape and balance and reaches a satisfying conclusion.

The Steamboat (Magazine, February 1821 to December 1822; book 1822)

Galt's next magazine serial for Blackwood's, *The Steamboat*, has on the whole had a bad press. Francis Jeffrey in his essay on "Secondary Scotch Novels" in the *Edinburgh Review* (October 1823) said that it was "a series of vulgar stories" which had "really no merit at all". Later critics have tended either to agree with him or to ignore the book entirely. It is certainly a more relaxed and less polished performance than the *Annals* or even *The Ayrshire Legatees*, but it is highly entertaining for all that.

In form, *The Steamboat* is another first-person narrative, the account of some jaunts down the Clyde and to London and back by Mr Duffle, a cloth merchant of Glasgow. This is used as a framework to string a number of miscellaneous stories in a variety of styles which are, improbably, said to have been told to Mr Duffle by his fellow passengers. The centrepiece of the book is a highly irreverent account of the coronation of George IV. This was included presumably to satisfy the curiosity of the readers of Blackwood's about royal occasions in the remote metropolis, but it also gave Galt an opportunity to express his own feelings about "the tomfoolery of the coronation"[8] as he called it in *The Literary Life*. "It did more", he said, "to lessen my respect for the tricks of state than anything I ever witnessed."[9] He had to restrain the "ready levity" of his pen, but "the original sin may be detected here and there peeping out".[11] It can indeed.

Mr Duffle's connecting narrative is another of Galt's studies in ironic self-revelation, but much less highly developed than in the *Annals* or *The Provost*. He tells us very little about himself, but he constantly displays an impregnable naivety, which enables Galt to keep up a flow of sly, or more precisely, pawky comment on everything he sees. He describes the Custom-house at Greenock (where Galt began his working life) as "a stately erection, bearing a similitude to our jail".[11] Another joke at the expense of Greenock (which seems to have been one of Galt's favourites because he repeats it in *The Entail*) is the daft laddie saying "It's a fine place, for a' the folk are just like mysel' ".[12] As often in Galt, there is a good deal of teasing of the pretensions of Edinburgh. "It is well known that the Edinburgh folk are in the main a well-informed, civilised sort of people, though a thought gi'en, as we think in the West, to making mair rouse about themselves than there is any needcessity for."[13]

On his voyage to London, Mr Duffle has the good fortune to fall in with Dr and Mrs Pringle of *The Ayrshire Legatees* (one of Galt's innumerable cross-references). They are going to London on the pretext of their daughter's, now Mrs Sabre's, confinement, but also, although like Mr Duffle they are reluctant to admit it, because they are drawn by curiosity over the coronation. Their presbyterian disapproval of the "great palavering of priesthood and heraldry"[14] is joined to Mr Duffle's own. They sympathise with the King's predicament in finding himself exposed to all of this. "But it's no new thing for Kings to be ill served", Mr Duffle reflects, "and our Majesty might by this time, I think, have been used to the misfortune—considering what sort of men his ministers are."[15] Mr Duffle's conclusion is that the annual coronation of King Crispin by the shoemakers of Glasgow is a far finer show all together, as well as cheaper, "But this is not to be wondered at, considering how much more experience the craft have".[16] All of this can be read as a comedy of the innocent abroad, neither understanding nor appreciating what he is seeing; but it is also a strong, and very Scottish, deflation of ostentation and sham.

Real people as well as characters from the other novels make an appearance. Mrs Pringle, for instance, notices:

> An elderly man, about fifty, with a fair gray head, and something of the appearance of a gausey good humoured country laird. "That's the Author of *Waverley* ... a most comical novel that the doctor read, and thought was a true history book."[17]

The inserted stories are a mixed bag. Many of them are quite slight, and some are left unfinished on the pretext that the steamboat has reached the narrator's destination. They demonstrate Galt's ability to make the language fit the speaker, and he experiments with a number of varieties of English in addition to his Scots. Although one of the early stories, "The Soldier's Mother", strikes a note of controlled pathos, most of them are extended jokes. Some critics have reacted to some of these with disproportionate pomposity. "A Jeannie Deans in Love", for instance, has really given more offence by its title than its content. The reaction to "Mrs Ogle of Balbogle" is the most extraordinary of all. This is an amusing account of a practical joke which actually happened to Francis Jeffrey when a high-spirited girl of his acquaintance kept him from his dinner guests by acting the part of a masterful and loquacious woman of the type of Galt's Mrs Soorocks from *The Last of the Lairds*. The story is good-natured fun, with only the slightest of gibes at Jeffrey, "he's no without a share of common sense, though aiblins a wee conceity of himself". Lockhart set the tone of disapproval in a letter to Blackwood: "Mrs Ogle is exquisite . . . but nobody has the right to meddle with the private affairs of a private lady".[18] This is the primness of the age of gentility at the most far-fetched. It is curious to find it still echoed in the 20th century, when R. K. Gordon calls the story, "inexcusable indulgence in personalities".[19]

The Gathering of the West: or We're Come to See the King (Magazine, September 1822; book 1823)

Galt spent the summer of 1822 in Scotland when he was writing *The Entail* and wanted to refresh his vernacular vocabulary at its source. He spent August in Edinburgh, and was there during the notorious visit of George IV. Blackwood seized the opportunity to press him to write an article for his magazine. The result, *The Gathering of the West*, took up about 30 pages of the September issue. It was an exuberant piece of high-spirited comedy with a satirical edge.

Irony always involves the risk of misunderstanding. Bradford Booth, who edited an edition of the text in 1939, fell completely into the trap. Galt, he tells us in his Preface, "is proud of the respect with which the Scottish people treated their King. Having recently witnessed the ludicrous and even disgusting ceremonies of the coronation, he was delighted with the reverend homage paid royalty at Edinburgh."[20] This is the precise opposite of Galt's reaction and of his intention in the sketch, but in a strange way it is also an unconscious tribute to his skill. Galt was walking a tight-rope in expressing what he really felt about the visit in such a way that Blackwood and royalists among the readers of the Magazine would, like Booth, take it at literal face value.

It is true that Galt made a clear distinction between the events in Edinburgh and London. The coronation and the behaviour of the guests after the coronation ceremony had disgusted and amused him. "If anything were calculated to inspire laughable contempt for the melo-drama of earthly grandeur, it was the hurly-burly in Westminster Hall subsequent to the King's departure."[21] In Edinburgh there was one incident from which he "derived entire pleasure". This was when the King went in state to St Giles on the Sabbath. "A countless multitude crowded the pavement, but the royal cortège was allowed to pass along in silence, the spectators only uncovering respectfully as it passed. Nothing could have given me a higher notion of the good sense of my countrymen."[22] But the crowd was not always so sensible. "If the coronation disclosed the folly that sits in high places, the gathering to see the King in Edinburgh fully matched it, by showing the depths of absurdity to which the mass will descend."[23] As with *The Steamboat* he was anxious "not to be offensive to those who enjoyed the show; but somehow so many ludicrous objects fascinated my attention that it was very difficult to be serious".[24]

The emphasis in *The Gathering of the West* is therefore on the way the visit went to people's heads, not on the official events themselves, although we have Henry Mackenzie's word for it that Galt recorded every event exactly as it occurred.[25] The book begins in his own country in the West, where Greenock burghers and especially their wives, radical Paisley weavers and Glasgow bailies are caught up in the enthusiasm of the occasion and make the pilgrimage to Edinburgh. The weavers, for a time at least, abjure reform. The Senate of Glasgow University display "their orthodox respect for Presbyterian simplicity" in coats of "sumptuous purple velvet, dyed to the right Archiepiscopal hue".[26] The Provost rides to Edinburgh in a coach which Galt compares to Cleopatra's golden barge, with "before him two pretty dimpled bailies, like smiling Cupids. O rare for Edinburgh!"[27]

In Edinburgh itself, attention turns to the efforts of the

two Greenock couples to vie with one another in seeing the sights and especially the King himself, an objective which they just manage to achieve. Characters from Galt's earlier books and some real people jostle with them. The sketch becomes domestic comedy, heightening the mockery of the whole event. Galt was fond of referring to his novels in a self-deprecatory way as clishmaclavers, in the sense of idle talk or gossip. This is a good example of his clishmaclaver style. Much of the book is in dialogue, and indeed it begins by plunging straight into one without any preliminary matter, like Sterne in *A Sentimental Journey*. This is now, of course, a familiar device, but it was rare at the time and is another instance of Galt's continual experiment with narrative technique.

Galt makes no reference to the symbolic significance which is often seen in the visit as a reconciliation between Scotland and the Hanoverians and between Highlander and Lowlander. He makes only one reference to the tartan enthusiasm: "writers and writers' clerks were seen trembling in the breeze, dressed in the Celtic garb, that their peeled, white, ladylike legs might acquire the healthy complexion of Highland boughs".[28] Perhaps these matters only seemed important in retrospect long after the event; or were inconsistent with Galt's immediate purpose. Walter Scott, who largely stage-managed the whole affair, makes only a marginal appearance as the Baronet, but Galt includes a parody, said to issue from "Blackwood's Emporium of Loyalty, Literature and Libels" of Scott's song, "Carle, Now the King's Come".[29] Jeffrey again appears as Mr Jamphrey, "just the very suckling wet nurse to every writer of books, and nothing gave him more satisfaction than to say pleasant things of those who stood in need of praise".[30]

Galt described *The Gathering of the West* as a "mere occasional *jeu d'esprit*".[31] So it is, but it is also one of his wittiest and most entertaining performances.

REFERENCES

1. Tobias Smollett: *Humphry Clinker* (1771) World's Classic edition (1938), pp. 338–45.
2. A.L., Chapt. IV—Following Letter X.
3. A.L., Chapt. IV—Letter IX.
4. A.L., Chapt. IV—Letter IX.
5. Aut., Vol. II, p. 229.
6. A.L., Chapt. VI.
7. A.L., Chapt. X.
8. L.L., Vol. I, p. 237.
9. L.L., Vol. I, p. 240.
10. L.L., Vol. I, p. 236.
11. Sb., p. 54.
12. Sb., p. 127.
13. Sb., p. 337.
14. Sb., p. 204.
15. Sb., p. 203.
16. Sb., pp. 207–8.
17. Sb., p. 253.
18. Oliphant: Vol. I, p. 218.
19. R. K. Gordon: *John Galt* (1920), p. 31.
20. B. A. Booth: Introduction to his edition of *The Gathering of the West* (1939), p. 34.
21. L.L., Vol. I, p. 239.
22. L.L., Vol. I, p. 242.
23. L.L., Vol. I, p. 240.
24. L.L., Vol. I, p. 236.
25. *The Anecdotes and Egotisms of Henry Mackenzie*, edited H. W. Thompson (1927), p. 13.
26. Gath., p. 59.
27. Gath., p. 58.
28. Gath., p. 66.
29. Gath., pp. 88–9.
30. Gath., p. 100.
31. L.L., Vol. I, p. 242.

CHAPTER V

THE PROVOST (1822)

"The Provost", Galt said in his *Literary Life*, "was intended to be a companion to the *Annals of the Parish*. The latter exhibited the progress of improvement in a rural district of the West of Scotland; and I proposed, in the former, to describe the same process in a town."[1] As companion pieces, the two books have a great deal in common. Both are fictitious first-person narratives of convincing actuality. They cover much the same period. This is explicit in the *Annals* where each chapter is dated. *The Provost* mentions few dates, but they can be implied from the references to the American Wars about the middle of the book and to the Battle of Waterloo in the last chapter. The two settings are very close together also in distance. Dreghorn, the original of Dalmailing, is only two miles outside Irvine, which is the Gudetown of *The Provost*. The two books are even of about the same length, each with about fifty fairly short chapters.

At the same time, each of the books is quite distinct in atmosphere. The narrator of one is a country minister and of the other a small-town magistrate. Galt gives each of them a personality shaped by, and entirely appropriate to, his calling and with habits of speech and style to match. In both books this is sustained consistently from beginning to end. There is hardly a sentence of Mr Balwhidder of the *Annals* which could be mistaken for one of Mr Pawkie of *The Provost*. Mr Balwhidder's prose has a gentle, leisurely quality, with a simplicity qualified by biblical and literary overtones. His faith and piety are so much taken for granted that they are evident without his having to insist upon them. The man and the style are inseparable. Mr Pawkie is a man of very different background, character and experience, and this is apparent from every remark he makes. He is self-interested and self-made, brisk, efficient and energetic, jocose, shrewd and used to manipulating his fellow townsmen. He radiates self-confidence and self-esteem with no trace of the diffidence and self-questioning of Mr Balwhidder. He is as calculating and ambitious as Mr Balwhidder is passive and unworldly. His prose echoes all of this. It is sharper and brisker than Mr Balwhidder's and blunter and earthier in tone, but with touches of the pomposity of the dignitary and the rotundity of the council chamber. He is a master of pungent Scots phrase: "outgait and blether in the causey", "with a grand stot and strut".[2] It is impossible to read one of these books after the other without being impressed by Galt's ability to sustain an entirely credible impersonation without a false note from one end of the narrative to another. The distinctiveness within the general similarity of the two books is the measure of his skill.

The two men have one thing in common. They both take their own communities and their role in them very seriously. Part of the obvious comedy lies in their lack of a sense of proportion. Mr Balwhidder could compare himself to the king, but he did see that his parish was a "narrow sphere". Mr Pawkie goes further. He sets the tone in the very first paragraph of his account by writing of himself in grandiloquent terms more like a prime minister than a provost:

> It must be allowed in the world, that a man who has thrice reached the highest station in life, in his line, has a good right to set forth the particulars of the discretion and prudence by which he lifted himself so far above the ordinaries of his day and generation: indeed, the generality of mankind may claim this as a duty; for the conduct of public men, as it has been

often wisely said, is a species of public property, and their rules and observances have in all ages been considered things of a national concernment.

Mr Pawkie, true to his word, then proceeds to tell us how he manipulated his way to the "whole sway and mastery of the town".[3] He feathers his nest as he goes, and never falters in the esteem of his fellow citizens or of his own. He is the consummate politician, a master of every trick in the book.

Galt tells us that he had a model for Mr Pawkie, a certain Bailie Fullarton, "I had in view, while writing it, a gentleman, who, when I was a boy at school, had the chief management of the borough council in my native town. He was unblemished in reputation, with considerable talent for his sphere, and, it was alleged, possessed that pawkie art, in which the hero is delineated to have excelled. . . . I believed he was dead, and had no scruple about him for my model."[4] But Bailie Fullarton, like Mr Pawkie, was clearly one of nature's survivors. Thirty years after he left Irvine, and three years after he published *The Provost*, Galt was invited back to his native place to receive the freedom of the burgh. And who should be presiding over the proceedings but the same Bailie Fullarton. "His speech partook of his character, and evinced a degree of good sense, a tact, and taste, though delivered in the Scottish dialect, quite extraordinary. . . . Provost Pawkie himself could never have said anything half so good."[5]

Unfortunately, we do not know what Bailie Fullarton thought about *The Provost*. Presumably he would not have presided over a ceremony in Galt's honour if he had recognised that the book was a satire on him and his kind. Galt betrays no embarrassment over the encounter. Should we perhaps think again about the ironic self-revelation, for which the book has always been praised?

The key word is obviously pawkie: "that pawkie art in which the hero is delineated to have excelled". The difficulty is that the word, as the examples in the *Scottish National Dictionary* abundantly demonstrate, has a variety of meanings and nuances which range from the derogatory to the complimentary. It can mean "wily, shy, cunning, crafty", but also "shrewd, astute, sagacious, sharp, resourceful". It can also mean "self-satisfied, proud, vain", but also "roguish, arch, vivacious, jaunty". Perhaps most often it means "characterised by a sly, quiet wit, quizzical, sardonic, having a matter-of-fact, humorously critical outlook on life". Mr Pawkie is all of these things at once, which is an indication of how beautifully apposite the word is. On the whole, the word is generally more of a compliment than otherwise. It covers many of the qualities likely to win popularity and success, in Scotland at least, a mixture of sagacity, wit, directness and psychological insight.

In fact, Galt's portrait of Mr Pawkie is by no means entirely unsympathetic. He is successful because he deserves to be, because of his intelligence, application and understanding of human motives. He keeps a careful eye on his public image and is more concerned about the reality of power than in outward show. He is benevolent and good natured. Galt was not setting up an easy satirical target of a man with only negative qualities; his Mr Pawkie is much more complex. On the reverse side, he is impregnably self-satisfied, always lining his own purse and subservient to superior authority. All of this Mr Pawkie reveals apparently without realising how much he is giving away. Would a man as shrewd as he is be so indiscreet and is there therefore a basic improbability in Galt's technique of ironic self-revelation? It seems to me that is a measure of Galt's ingenuity that the self revelation is a necessary and inherent part of Mr Pawkie's character. He is so self-satisfied that he has to boast about his achievements and he is taken in by his own justifications. It is a type of character not unknown among politicians. Perhaps Galt succeeded so well that Bailie Fullarton himself was deluded in exactly the same way as Mr Pawkie.

Keith Costain in his essay on the book, "The Prince and the Provost",[6] treats it as a savage satire. Others have seen it in a more amiable light, as a shrewd but not unforgiving analysis of attributes and devices that normally accompany the achievement and exercise of power at any level. John Wilson took this view: "Provost Pawkie is not a perfect character, although a loyal good Tory. He is so base and corrupted as to be occasionally influenced by motives of self-interest, more especially when they coincide with a regard to the public good. . . . Long may our bouroughs have such bailies and such provosts as the late esteemed Mr Pawkie."[7] S. R. Crockett agreed: "The Provost is by no means such a vile and heartless Machiavelli as Balzac would have drawn. . . . The world would not be so very badly governed if all rulers and magistrates were no worse than the excellent Provost of Gudetown."[8] It seems to me that Galt's book is indeed more an attack on the system than on the man.

Apart from Bailie Fullarton's reaction, there is good evidence that *The Provost* is a faithful account of the life of the 18th-century Irvine. In the notes to his excellent edition (Oxford, 1973) Ian Gordon has shown how nearly every episode in the book can be traced in the Burgh Minute Books. Of course, Galt, who wrote the book far from Irvine, was not relying on the official minutes. There is no reason to suppose that he ever consulted them. He was relying on his observations in his childhood and his memory of local gossip. The sparse entries in the Minutes are given flesh and blood in Galt's account. A good example is the episode of the drunken town drummer, Robin Boss. The Minute Books record three occasions when the drummer had to be replaced because he was "unfit for his duty",[9] leaving the details to the imagination. Galt gives life to the event as well as implying some conclusions on the conduct of public business. *The Provost* no less than the *Annals* is an accurate picture of a slice of

18th-century Scottish life, and is even more detailed and circumstantial because it was closer to Galt's own experience.

Like the *Annals* too, *The Provost* is also concerned with change, although Mr Pawkie lays less emphasis on it than Mr Balwhidder. They have a different point of view. Mr Balwhidder was a largely passive observer with leisure to look around and take an interest in everything. Mr Pawkie was actively involved in the affairs of the Burgh. Paradoxically, but it follows from the character of the two men, Mr Balwhidder's view of change is the more comprehensive; he noted everything from agricultural improvement and industrialisation to the effects of foreign wars and the spread of new ideas. For the most part, Mr Pawkie tells us about the small matters of local government, street lighting and paving, the repair of the Kirk, the suppression of the fairs. Certainly, he also notices the changes in the intellectual and political climate, but he judges them from the effects on his own conduct of business. He sees that it was a "new era in public affairs" when people "should dare to question and interfere with the magistrates". Accordingly, he squared his conduct "more by a deference to public opinion"[10] and his influence in the community grew in strength in consequence. He "had lived to partake of the purer spirit which the great mutations of the age had conjured into public affairs".[11] Again he adjusts, although that does not stop him accepting discreet bribes from both candidates in a Parliamentary election. He records the decline of the country gentry, because they had started to condescend to take an interest in the affairs of the Burgh, "the bit prideful lairdies were just looked down upon by our gausie big-bellied burgesses, not a few of whom had heritable bonds on their estates".[12] A newspaper is founded to promote liberal principles, but by "a canny seduction of policy", he soon reduces it to "a very solid and decent supporter of the government".[13]

If this more self-centred view of change reflects the difference in character and role of the narrator, it also reflects a difference in the underlying theme of the book. The *Annals* was concerned with the nature of economic and social change and, I suggest, with the theories of Adam Ferguson about it. *The Provost* dealt in change certainly, but the emphasis was on the exercise of political power and influence. In 1814 Galt had written a magazine article, "instructions on the Art of Rising in the World", which was much influenced by his reading of Machiavelli. He tells us that when he first read *The Prince* he at first thought that it was "an odious collection of state maxims", but changed his mind when he began to see it as an "incomparable satire". He was delighted with the idea that Machiavelli "only recommended those things to be adopted by Statesmen which the worthies themselves have in all ages been ever dabbling in".[14] His theme in *The Provost* was the same, but in the form of a "fable to illustrate philosophical truths". The book is a prolonged demonstration of the arts by which Mr Pawkie "maintained an outward show of humility and moderation"[15] and learned "to rule without being felt, which is the great mystery of policy".[16] The setting is the small stage of the burgh council, but Galt was analysing the methods which might be used in any organisation that can be manipulated for the exercise of power. The book is a satirical comedy, but it is also a treatise on the realities of politics.

At the same time, Mr Pawkie's view of social change is not inconsistent with Ferguson's theory. As much as Mr Pawkie demonstrates his mastery of the affairs of his burgh he also recognises that he is only a pawn in the face of the great wave of change that no individual had planned or foreseen but which conditions the atmosphere in which he had to work. He sees that the "great mutations of the age" had brought with them a more democratic spirit and less tolerance of easy-going corruption. Whether he likes it or not, he has to accommodate himself to them. His repeated insistence that there was no conflict between the public interest and his own private gain has strong overtones of Adam Smith. No less than Mr Balwhidder he was illustrating the "philosophical truths" of the Scottish Enlightenment.

The Council in which Mr Pawkie exercised his talents was one of the self-perpetuating local oligarchies which controlled the burghs before the Reform Act. Lord Cockburn's celebrated description of the Edinburgh Town Council of the period might be applied to it:

> Within this Pandemonium sat the town-council, omnipotent, corrupt, impenetrable. Nothing was beyond its grasp; no variety of opinion disturbed its unanimity, for the pleasure of Dundas was the sole rule for every one of them. Reporters, the fruit of free discussion, did not exist; and though they had existed, would not have dared to disclose the proceedings. Silent, powerful, submissive, mysterious, and irresponsible, they might have been sitting in Venice.[17]

Cockburn's *Memorials* were not published until 1856, but here was Galt in 1822, ten years before the Reform Act, writing a ruthless exposure of the unreformed administration. He did not confine himself to local government, but in the chapters on Parliamentary elections also showed how the restricted electorate inevitably encouraged corruption and abuse. To write such a book was an extraordinary activity for a self-professed Tory and it is even stranger that it should have been published by William Blackwood, a publisher devoted to the Tory cause. It is, of course, impossible to know how much effect to book had on public opinion, although it must have tended to undermine support for the political *status quo*. It certainly sold well. *Blackwood's* reported in June 1822, a month after the publication, that the first edition of 2,000 copies had gone in a fortnight and that the second edition was melting away "like snaw off a dyke". Galt was pleased that George Canning read the book during a "dull debate" in the House of Commons and "spoke of it afterwards always with commendation".[18] Canning was the ablest opponent of parliamentary reform, but is said to have been moving towards it before his death in 1827.[19] Perhaps he, and others, were influenced by *The Provost*. It is a very effective piece of polemical writing, although that aspect of it does not seem to have attracted much comment.

Galt himself thought that *The Provost* was superior to the *Annals*.[20] It was highly praised by Coleridge, with an allusion also to Wordsworth, in a marginal note on his own copy of the book:

> This work is not for the Many; but in the unconscious, perfectly natural, Irony of Self-delusion, in all parts intelligible to the intelligent Reader, without the slightest suspicion on the part of the Autobiographer, I know of no equal in our Literature. The governing Trait in the Provost's character is no where carica- tured. In the character of Betty, John's wife, or the Beggar Girl intense selfishness without malignity, as a *Nature*, and with all the innocence of a Nature, is admirably pourtrayed. In the Provost a similar *Selfness* is united with a *Slyness* and a plausibility eminently successful in cheating the man himself into a happy state of constant Self-applause. This and "The Entail" would alone suffice to place Galt in the first rank of contemporary Novelists—and second only to Sir Walter Scott in technique.[21]

This is precise comment which hits the nail exactly on the head, but had Coleridge read *Annals of the Parish*? It seems to me that in that book Galt used the "irony of self-delusion" with greater subtlety, variety and humanity. In *The Provost*, from the character of the subject, it is restricted to one or two themes and driven home more obviously by repetition. The greatest strength of *The Provost* lies

elsewhere. It is one of the first political novels and is still
one of the most sharply observed.

REFERENCES

1. L.L., Vol. 1, p. 255.
2. Pro., Chapt. IX & Chapt. XXXIX.
3. Pro., Chapt. XXV.
4. Aut., Vol. II, p. 231.
5. Aut., Vol. II, p. 232.
6. K. M. Costain in *Studies in Scottish Literature*, Vol. VI, No. I (1968).
7. John Wilson (Christopher North): "Letter of Thanks from an Occasional Contributor", *Blackwood's Magazine*, Vol. XI, June 1822, p. 743.
8. S. R. Crockett: Introduction to *The Provost*—Collected Edition of 1895/6, pp. XVII & XIX.
9. Ian G. Gordon: note to p. 101 in his edition of *The Provost* (1973).
10. Pro., Chapt. XXVIII.
11. Pro., Chapt. XLIII.
12. Pro., Chapt. XXXIV.
13. Pro., Chapt. XXXIX.
14. L.L., Vol. I, p. 161.
15. Pro., Chapt. II.
16. Pro., Chapt. III.
17. Henry Cockburn: *Memorials of His Time* (Ed. of 1872), p. 83.
18. Aut., Vol. II, p. 231.
19. *Encyclopaedia Britannica* (1967 edition), Vol. 4, p. 787.
20. Aut., Vol. II, p. 231.
21. *Times Literary Supplement* (letter from A. J. Ashley), 25 September 1930.

CHAPTER VI

TWO THREE-VOLUME NOVELS

Sir Andrew Wylie and *The Entail*

Sir Andrew Wylie of That Ilk (1822)

Galt's original intention with *Sir Andrew Wylie of That Ilk* was to write a "sketch", of a similar shape and size to the *Annals* or *The Provost*, of "the rise and progress of a Scotchman in London": Like these, it would have the coherence of a single theme without the artificiality of a contrived plot. He was persuaded by William Blackwood to expand it to the three volumes which was at the time standard for novels. to give it "a beginning, a middle and an end" and to introduce a diversity of episodes likely to meet the popular taste.[1] Galt did his best to meet the specification, but he knew that when he "worked with a story, it was in comparatively galling harness".[2] Some years later he wrote bluntly to Blackwood: "Sir Andrew Wylie, the most original of all I have ever done was spoilt by your interference".[3]

Some idea of what the book might have been like can be seen in the first ten chapters, which deal with Andrew's upbringing in Ayrshire, and last twenty, when he returns full of riches and honours. They are in Galt's best "Tales of the West" manner, although the book is in the third and not the first person. The characters have all the life, credibility and gift for the pungent phrase of the *Annals* or *The Provost*, with similar undertones of a changing social pattern, and the "improved spirit of the age".[4] For the first time, Galt sketches in detail one of the decaying lairds who had hovered in the background of the earlier books. He was Craiglands, "a carle that daunered about the doors wi' his hands in his pouches, and took them out at meal-time".[5] He was discovered after his death to have written "a most full account of all manner of particularities anent the decay of the ancient families of the west country",[6] a hint of *The Last of the Lairds* that Galt was to write four years later.

The early chapters are clearly autobiographical because they have an obvious similarity to Galt's account of his own childhood. Andrew was "a small and delicate child", mild in manner, "droll and whimsical" and "naturally shrewd and observant"—all phrases that might be applied to Galt himself. He acquired "a happy vernacular phraseology, which he retained through life, and which, with those who had a true relish of character, was enjoyed as something as rare and original as the more elegant endowment of genius".[7] He had a strong Scottish partiality. "Andrew was deeply versed in those honourable traditions which exalt the affections of Scottish patriotism so highly, that, even with the eyes of manhood, the Scotchman is rarely to be found, who, with all that travel and experience teach to the contrary, will not contend for the superiority of the national monuments of his native land—to say nothing whatever of the superior excellence of her institutions."[8]

The bulk of the book describes Andrew's meteoric rise to wealth, a parliamentary seat and a baronetcy, and is therefore closer to Galt's aspirations than to his experiences. But Andrew, like Galt, eventually retires to his native country. Here again, something of Galt's own feelings come through. "I have ever looked to taking my rest among the scenes of my young days; for still, in my thought, the mornings there are brighter than I have seen in any other place—the evenings far grander, and the nights thicker set with stars."[9] He was "firm in his intention to promote the welfare of his native country".[10]

Between this beginning and end, Galt packs in almost

every imaginable ingredient of the popular novel. There are elements, though restrained, both of the novel of sensibility and the gothic. Lord Sandyford has touches of the Byronic hero, and the novel moves into aristocratic society in the elaborate sub-plot of his marital misunderstandings. This is counterpoised with Andrew's own love story as the local boy who makes good and marries the laird's daughter. Like Sir Walter Scott, Galt brings in a band of gipsies. Even curiosity about royal personages is satisfied in episodes where Andrew meets the King. Anticipating a new kind of popular novel, there is a murder, detection and trial. There is political satire of the pre-reform manipulation and sale of parliamentary seats. All of this is held together by a series of wildly improbable coincidences. Students of the popular novel will find *Sir Andrew Wylie* a rich field for investigation. Galt both resumes established patterns and innovates others.

Throughout this astonishing clamjamfry of themes, Galt does not lose sight of his main subject, "the rise and progress of a Scotchman in London". With his own unhappy experience of the matter, Galt might have written a valuable and realistic account of the strains, tensions, misunderstandings and readjustment involved in the confrontation of two traditions. He had touched on this in *The Ayrshire Legatees*. Instead, in *Sir Andrew Wylie*, he indulged in a fantasy of wishful thinking without a hint of his customary irony. Andrew never loses either his vigorous Scottish speech or his Scottish habit of saying directly and bluntly what he means. He tells all and sundry exactly where they are going wrong and what they should do about it. You expect him to be thrown down the stairs as an impertinent upstart. On the contrary, everyone reacts like Lady Sandyford. "She could not but acknowledge in her own mind that he was undoubtedly endowed by nature with singular shrewdness, and with peculiar talents of no ordinary kind. It was true, that he said things which a delicate respect for the prejudices and notions of others would have restrained a man of more gentlemanly pretensions from expressing; but there was no resisting the strong common sense of his remarks, nor withstanding the good-humoured merriment of his allusions."[11] In consequence, he soars in no time to wealth, social prestige and political influence. Writing in *Blackwood's Magazine* when the book first appeared John Wilson made the point well: "He no sooner shows his face in company, high or low, than he ups with the first fiddle and leads the band.... Everyone listens to him, and acts on his advice. The Admirable Crichton, who was six feet six inches high ... and could speak twenty languages, would have been a mere Cypher in company with the wonderful Wylie, who stood only five foot two, on his stocking soles, and could speak no languages at all."[12] Galt, the social realist, had abandoned realism for a Walter Mitty dream.

But not entirely. In spite of all the absurdity, there are passages in *Sir Andrew Wylie* of sharp observation, and not exclusively in the admirable Ayrshire scenes. Lord Blessington, who did not realise that he was the model for Lord Sandyford, told Galt that his characters "must be very natural, for, in the same circumstances, he would have acted in a similar manner".[13] He speaks of acting not of speaking and that may have been deliberate because it is difficult to believe that anyone ever spoke in the stilted and artificial manner that Galt attributed to Lord Sandyford. George IV remarked of Galt's description of his predecessor that it was "by far the likest portrait of his majesty he had ever seen".[14] There are many other characters and episodes that have the ring of truth. *Sir Andrew Wylie* is a curate's egg of a book, but it is still worth reading. Not surprisingly perhaps, it was for some years the most popular of Galt's books in England.

The Entail (1822)

Galt's next three-volume novel, *The Entail*, was published in the same year as *Sir Andrew Wylie*, but it was a

book of a very different kind and indeed quite different
from anything else that Galt had attempted. It has some
incongruous characters and episodes towards the end, but
it was not a book artificially prolonged beyond its natural
length. It was a book conceived on a large scale, with an
emotional depth and sense of tragedy that needed space to
evolve. Galt's contemporaries immediately recognised its
virtues. Coleridge and Byron praised it and both Byron
and Scott read it three times. It is Balzacian in its intensity
and has often been compared to *Eugénie Grandet* or *Le Père
Goriot*.

The setting in place and time is roughly the same as the
Annals or *The Provost*. Most of the action takes place in the
estate of Kittlestoneheugh a few miles south of Glasgow or
in Glasgow itself. Claud Walkinshaw, the central character, was born a year before the Darien Expedition sailed
and therefore about 1697. His wife, with whose death the
book ends, was then in her seventies. The early years of
Claud's life are discussed in the first three chapters and the
book really only gets under way when he is already middle-
aged. The action of the book is therefore once again spread
over the second half of the 18th century. It deals with the
affairs of the Walkinshaw family over three generations
and it is accordingly an early example of the family
chronicle type of novel.

Throughout the "Tales of the West", Galt had shown
little sympathy with the lairds as a class and no patience
with their pretensions of family pride. They are invariably
shown as a class in decay, impoverished and ineffective, and, as Andrew Wylie says of Craiglands, "knotted
and knarled with obsolete prejudices".[15] Galt allows
Craigland's daughter to introduce some improvements in
the estate, but otherwise he does less than justice to the role
which many of the lairds in fact played in agricultural and
industrial innovation. In Galt's view, the lairds are
irrelevant, if not obstructive, and their place in society
is increasingly passing to the up and coming men of

commerce. It was partly, says Provost Pawkie, due to the "French Revolution, whereby men of substance thought it an expedient policy to relax in their ancient maxims of family pride and consequence; and partly to the great increase and growth of wealth which the influx of trade caused throughout the Kingdom, whereby the merchants were enabled to vie and ostentate even with the better sort of lairds".[16]

The plot of *The Entail* turns on the efforts of Claud Walkinshaw, an impoverished descendant of such a family, to recover the lands of his ancestors and secure them intact by every device of the law for his descendants. We are told in the first sentence of the book that he "was the sole surviving male heir of the Walkinshaws of Kittlestoneheugh". His grandfather had risked more than the whole value of his estate in the Darien scheme and his father had died on the expedition. Claud grew up in Glasgow, a penniless orphan in care of an old family servant. She filled his head with ideas of the "hereditary grandeur of his ancestors" and constantly urged him to recover the lands which the family had lost. This Claud sets out to do. He gradually scrapes together some money by working for years as a packman in the Borders, and then sets himself up as a cloth merchant in Glasgow. Eventually he is prosperous enough to buy the farm of Grippy, part of the old family estate. He resolves to marry and to entail the property on his children so that it would never again pass out of the control of his descendants.

At this point, the main action of the novel begins. Claud pursues his objective of acquiring more land and securing its succession intact in the family with a single-mindedness that excludes all other feelings and considerations. He marries a woman he detests because she is the heiress of a neighbouring laird. "Heaven may forgive the aversion I had to her, but my own nature never can!", as he afterwards confesses in a fit of remorse.[17] To keep the inheritance together, he has to exclude his eldest son,

Charles, in favour of the second, the half-witted Watty. The apparent success of his incessant and secretive contriving gives Claud no satisfaction. He has become the victim of an obsession which becomes an end in itself and gives him no peace. "I sold my soul to the Evil One in my childhood, that I might recover the inheritance of my forbears. Oh, the pride of that mystery! . . . I stifled the very sense o' loving-kindness within me."[18] The book becomes a study not of family pride, still less of avarice, but of obsession itself. Claud is tortured by a sense of guilt over the injustice to Charles, and when he dies he feels guilty of murder. His last-minute attempt to make retribution by providing for Charles's family is frustrated by his own death.

There is a marked change of atmosphere with Claud's death about half-way through the novel. So far, his obsession had given power and coherence to the book and he is by far the dominant character. Secondary attention is focussed on Watty, the supreme example of Galt's ability to combine pathos and comedy. Watty too disappears from the scene, shortly after the third son, George, contrives to have him declared fatuous by legal process, in pursuit of his own ambitions.

The second half of the novel is therefore deprived of the two men who had been the main characters so far, and for this reason alone loses pace and intensity. There is a coherence in the theme because the consequence of Claud's plotting and contrivance works its way through the next two generations, but Galt has already made his points about family pride, obsession and self-defeating egoism. To some extent, George follows in his father's footsteps in scheming to keep the family fortune in his own hands; but he is moved by commonplace greed and ambition, not by Claud's consuming and tragic obsession. The change of atmosphere is emphasised by a change of language. Galt, with historical accuracy, makes the new generation speak a fushionless and stilted English in place of the energetic

Scots of the earlier chapters. Also, perhaps trying to imitate Walter Scott, perhaps under pressure from William Blackwood, or perhaps simply trying to give more flavour to a flagging narrative, Galt introduces some incongruous and unsuccessful characters and episodes. His Mrs Eadie, the Highland wife of a Lowland Minister, seems to be an imitation of Scott's Norma in *The Pirate*. Her theatricality and second-sight, and the contrived coincidence of a ship-wreck which improbably suddenly brings characters together from all over Scotland have no place in a novel of ruthless realism.

Into this vacuum strides magnificently the figure of Girzy, Claud's widow and therefore known as Leddy Grippy. She had been overshadowed while Claud was alive, but she emerges luxuriantly in her new-found independence, triumphing both over her own imperfect understanding and all the ingenuity of the lawyers. She is shallow and self-centred, but open and spontaneous. Her egoism is tempered by generosity and affection, and it is not secretive and destructive like Claud's. For all her failings she is a life-enhancing force. Her flow of language is irresistible, with a rich vocabulary of Scots. Malapropisms rub shoulders with snatches of allusions to the Bible, proverbs, traditional songs and the law. She is an unconscious and inaccurate, but profuse, transmitter of traditional wisdom and oral literature. Above all, she is splendidly alive. Byron said that "the portraiture of Leddy Grippy was perhaps the most complete and original that had been added to the female gallery since the days of Shakespeare".[19]

Galt in his *Autobiography* and *Literary Life* says very little about the origins and intentions of *The Entail*, beyond remarking that it was based on the true story of a family which he had heard from the then Lord Provost of Glasgow, and which therefore "deserves to be considered as a kind of history in private life".[20] The atmosphere is markedly different from the other "Tales of the West". It is no less humorous, or even downright farcical in places, but the over-all tone is much more sombre. This lies not only in the emphasis on death and the fatuity of human aspirations, but in the much harsher view of character and behaviour. In the earlier books, Galt takes the Adam Ferguson view of human nature, that it is generally benevolent, sociable and neighbourly. In *The Entail* there are characters who have few redeeming qualities and are entirely self-centred and selfish. They have very little benevolence even towards members of their own family, to say nothing of the community at large. As a picture of family life, it is almost brutal in its realism.

Because the plot of *The Entail* turns on a legal device, the law and lawyers play a large part, and several of the other characters, including Leddy Grippy, fancy themselves as amateur lawyers. The professionals range from the upright and well-intentioned Mr Keelevin to some rogues out for a quick killing. From the constant allusions to the law and the necessary interventions of lawyers at almost every decisive turning in the story, the law itself becomes a theme of the book. Galt seems deliberately to be making a contrast between law and justice. This reflects one of Galt's personal convictions. R. P. Gillies, in his recollections of Galt, says that "in his opinion legal power was one thing, but right or justice another".[21] When Charles is disinherited, it is good law but bad justice. A verdict of fatuity is declared on Watty by a jury and all the panoply of judicial enquiry, but is contrived for reasons which have nothing to do with justice. The final triumph of justice is due more to Leddy Grippy's intuitional interference than to the system of law.

Galt's account of the material recovery of the fortunes of the Walkinshaw family is not inconsistent with the general picture of the decline of the lairds. The money with which Claud begins the process comes from commerce. As his prospective father-in-law remarks, "Glasgow's on the thrive",[22] and it remains the chief source of wealth. The

Walkinshaws have, in effect, themselves become part of the new commercial class who were displacing the traditional laird with his income derived from rents on agricultural land.

The Entail, and from the nature of the plot it could hardly be otherwise, is told in the third person by a narrator who is generally but not always, invisible. Galt occasionally makes him, Hitchcock-like, appear on the margins of the action. Perhaps by these unobtrusive touches Galt hoped to achieve the verisimilitude of his fictitious autobiographies, but they are too infrequent, and too inconsistent with the narrator's omniscience, to have that effect.

Taken as a whole, *The Entail* does not match the *Annals* or *The Provost* in utter credibility. It does not have the perfection in their kind of these two books, which hardly have a superfluous page or one which might have been better. In tragic intensity, controlled pathos, verbal exuberance and the comic inventiveness of Leddy Grippy, however, *The Entail* at its best has no parallel in Galt and very few in any other novelist.

REFERENCES

1. Aut., Vol. II, p. 239.
2. L.L., Col. I, p. 317.
3. *Times Literary Supplement*, 6 June 1942, p. 288.
4. A.W., Chapt. LXXXIX.
5. A.W., Chapt. II.
6. A.W., Chapt. CV.
7. A.W., Chapt. I.
8. A.W., Chapt. X.
9. A.W., Chapt. LXXXIII.
10. A.W., Chapt. CV.
11. A.W., Chapt. XXXV.
12. *Blackwood's Magazine*, Vol. XI, June 1822, pp. 742–3.
13. Aut., Vol. II, p. 239.

14. Aut., Vol. II, p. 276.
15. A.W., Chapt. CIII.
16. Pro., Chapt. XXXIV.
17. Ent., Chapt. XLIV.
18. Ent. Chapt. XLIV.
19. Jennie W. Aberdein: *John Galt* (1936), p. 122.
20. Aut., Vol. II, p. 238, and L.L., Vol. I, pp. 246–7.
21. R. P. Gillies: *op. cit.*, Vol. III, p. 60.
22. Ent., Chapt. IV.

CHAPTER VII

THE LAST OF THE LAIRDS (1826)

In the three years after the publication of *The Entail* in 1822, Galt was writing novels of a different kind for another Edinburgh publisher, Oliver and Boyd. In 1825, he returned to Blackwood's and started to write another novel about life in the West of Scotland, *The Last of the Lairds*. Apart from some short stories, it rounded off the series; *the Last of the Lairds* was also the last of the "Tales of the West". Even if it means breaking strict chronology, it obviously makes sense to look at it in the context of its companion pieces.

In his *Literary Life*, Galt explained what he was trying to do and expressed some disappointment with the result:

> I meant it to belong to that series of fictions of manners, of which the Annals of the Parish is the beginning; but owing to some cause, which I no longer remember, instead of an autobiography I was induced to make it a narrative, and in this respect it lost that appearance of truth and nature which is, in my opinion, the great charm of such works. I have no recollection how this happened, nor what caused me to write it as it is, but the experiment was a very unwise one, and some day I will try to supply what is wanted, namely the autobiography of one of the last race of lairds. But although the work lacks essentially in being a story, it ought to have been more amusing than it is, and yet it is not deficient in that kind of caricature which is at once laughable and true.[1]

This guarded but barbed account concealed a long struggle between Galt and William Blackwood. At first,

Blackwood was delighted with the idea that Galt would honour the promise at the end of *Sir Andrew Wylie* and write a history of the decay of an ancient family in the manner of the *Annals* or *The Provost*. As Galt's manuscript came in by instalments, however, Blackwood was increasingly alarmed by its directness and realism, its tendency to call a spade, a spade. His reaction was similar to Susan Ferrier's, another of his authors, who had said of *Sir Andrew Wylie*: "I can't endure that man's writing, and I am told the vulgarity of this beats print".[2] The same word "Vulgarity" occurs several times in Francis Jeffrey's otherwise largely favourable comments on Galt in his essay in the *Edinburgh Review* of October 1823. Perhaps it was this as much as anything which scared Blackwood. The trouble was that Blackwood, Susan Ferrier and people in influential places who thought like them, were increasingly succumbing to the dead hand of gentility, that baleful influence on 19th-century life and writing. Galt slips in some references to it in *The Last of the Lairds* itself. "May God forgive me", the narrator says at one point, "but this is an age much addicted to hypocrisy."[3] The Laird's man, Jack, says of the memoir which the Laird is struggling to write: "If it has a fault (and what has na?) it's a want o' gentility".[4] It was precisely this want of gentility which upset William Blackwood.

The row between writer and publisher was carried on in more than thirty letters between them, at a time when Galt was also busy with his preparations to leave for Canada. Finally time ran out and he left it to Blackwood's reader and collaborator, D. M. Moir to "carve and change as you please".[5] Moir bowdlerised and toned down the book and even lost Galt's delicately ironic ending by adding three new chapters of his own at the end. By a fortunate accident, the manuscript of all but the first eighteen chapters survived in Moir's family, and is now in the National Library of Scotland. We therefore, after 150 years, at last have a text free of Moir's emendations, in the edition

edited by Ian A. Gordon and published in 1976. Gordon's
footnotes to the text allow us to see what Blackwood and
Moir regarded as "vulgar". By 20th-century standards,
there was nothing very indecorous about Galt's manuscript. Moir's deletions and changes are mainly to passages
of mild sexual innuendo or even milder blasphemy. He
takes fright at the slightest hint of either to a degree which
now seems paranoiac. A reference to "petticoats kilted far
above her knees", even in so innocent a context as a servant
lassie in the washing tub, has him rushing for his blue
pencil. "The Lord in his displeasure" is changed to the
safer abstraction of "Heaven". The hilarious drunken
scene in Chapter XXXII is amended to avoid the
implication that it led to the Laird taking his bride to bed.
It is the prudery of Blackwood which is now astonishing,
not the outrageousness of Galt.

Galt's disappointment with the book as it was published
must refer to what Moir had made of it. Before that, he had
said in a letter to Blackwood: "My own feelings with respect to my work is that it is the first of all my writing, and
that the characters are marked out with more individuality than any of my other works. . . . In fact, the persons
came to my imagination as actual persons, and I could no
more change their method of thinking than I could those of
any living individuals."[6]

When Galt said that he was induced to abandon his
original idea of writing another fictional autobiography,
he meant of course in the person of the Laird himself and
taking in most of his life, like Mr Balwhidder or Provost
Pawkie. In fact, the book is written in the first person by a
narrator who is directly involved in the action. He is a
neighbour of the Laird, but a man of very different type, a
writer who is in touch with the books and literary gossip of
the age. He shares with another of the characters, Mrs
Soorocks, an urge to take an interest in the lives of their
neighbours and, in her phrase, "Scald my lips in other
folk's kail",[7] with each continually accusing the other of

the failing. We are in fact given a specimen of the memoir which the Laird, Malachi Mailings of Auldbriggings, is trying to write in a desperate attempt to pay off his debts. A sustained literary effort of this kind does not really suit his ineffective character. In his letter to Moir, Galt suggests that it was for this reason that he decided to cast the story in a different form.

The time-scale of the book is also very different from the fifty years or so of the *Annals* or *The Provost*. Most of the characters take us back in the past by an occasional reminiscence, but the action of the book (apart from the epilogue in the last couple of pages) all takes place within about three weeks.[8] It is firmly set in Galt's own time, as appears from many topical references. Geographically, it is in yet another corner of the Galt country; this time close to Paisley. Instead of the whole life-time of an autobiography, therefore, we have only the closing phase of Auldbigging's hold on his ancestral lands. Galt tells us that he moulded him on a laird, "who was alive in my boyhood",[9] but he is also representative of a whole class of west-country lairds "who are now extinct".[10]

The surprising thing about a book with such a troubled and acrimonious birth is that it is the most exuberantly farcical of all Galt's novels. Galt's own judgement, "that kind of caricature which is at once laughable and true" is just. Nearly all the characters are caricatures. Their foibles are exaggerated, but not to the point where they become merely grotesque. Mr Rupees, back in his native place after making his fortune in India, out-nabobs all the nabobs in literature. Mrs Soorocks, with a gift for the pungent Scots phrase only excelled by Leddy Grippy, is a supreme busybody. At the same time, they are perfectly credible as people with a mixture of motives and responses that become more involved as the story develops.

To the broad farce, Galt frequently adds ironic sallies at some of his favourite targets. In wet weather, the ducks are "as garrulous with enjoyment at the middenhole, as Tories

in the pools of corruption".[11] The whole episode of the
Laird's sale of his feudal superiority, in other words the
right to a vote, is another attack on the pre-Reform
electoral system. There are satirical asides about the
Literary Gazette and *Blackwood's Magazine* itself. He refers to
the Edinburgh literary establishment as "persons so self-
celebrated".[12] Even the brass plate on Auldbigging's
Edinburgh door gives Galt a chance to deflate the
pretentiousness of the legal fraternity: "That advocates
and writers to the signet should like other tradesmen have
recourse to such brazen devices to make themselves
notorious and to bring custom seems not unreasonable".[13]

What the book loses in intimacy in having a different
narrator from the Laird himself, it gains in detachment.
We see his predicament mainly through other eyes. At first,
the narrator is contemptuous. He refers to Auldbiggings as
an idiot and half resolves not to see him again. Before long,
his sympathies are fully engaged and he joins with his other
neighbours in doing their best to help. Auldbiggings
becomes a symbol of the old Scotland whose passing is a
matter for regret. The decline of his family is seen as part of
a process of change which began with the Union. "It was",
says Auldbiggings, "a black day for Scotland that saw the
Union signed."[14] The conflict between the old forces and
the new, represented by Mr Rupees, became the subject of
open but unresolved debate, in Chapter XVII. In the end,
Auldbiggings has to give way to Rupees, but with the
consolation of his triumph over the sale of the electoral
superiority. Throughout the book, an elegiac note of
sorrow at the passing of old ways underlines the comedy.

I have spoken of the "Tales of the West", as Galt did
himself, as though they were a homogeneous series of
books. It is true that they all deal with the same part of the
world and mostly with the period of time that could be
covered by living memory up to Galt's own day. Together
they form a comprehensive picture of the life of a wide
range of society as it evolved around Glasgow, Greenock

and Irvine in the seventy-odd years up to the 1820s. The
books are, however, not uniform in narrative technique,
style, atmosphere or theme. In all of these matters, Galt
was varied and inventive. The *Annals* and *The Provost* are
the most similar in technique, since they are both
imaginary autobiographies. Others have a first-person
narrator, self-effacing and at the margins of the action as in
The Entail or prominent and involved as in *The Last of the
Lairds*. The letters of *The Ayrshire Legatees* give a variety of
first-person accounts. *Sir Andrew Wylie* has an omniscient
third-person narrator. In style the books are as diverse as
the narrators. The themes, the nature and effect of social
change or the mechanism of power, are elaborately studied
in the *Annals* and *The Provost*, but less analytically in the
others. All the books combine comedy and pathos but in
varying degrees, from the sombre tone of the first half of
The Entail to the outrageous farce of *The Last of the Lairds*.
Not the least remarkable quality of this series of novels is
their diversity. In the course of this book I have found
myself comparing aspects of Galt to Defoe, Walter Scott,
Jane Austen and Balzac. Others have found similarities
with Zola,[15] Trollope,[16] Hardy,[17] Gogol and Dostoyevsky.[18] That is a measure of Galt's range.

From such a prolonged study of Scottish personality and
social behaviour, even if limited to one part of the country,
Galt has seemed to some people to offer a composite picture
of the national character. Jane Findlater accused him of
establishing the "unpleasant popular idea of the Scottish
character".[19] This is an eccentric view. I think the
American, Ruth Aldrich is much closer to the truth when
she says that the outstanding trait that emerges is kindness
and concern for others.[20] The one prominent character
who stifles this feeling, Claud Walkinshaw, is tortured by
guilt precisely because he realises that this is what he has
done. This is essentially the Scottish Enlightenment view of
human nature from Francis Hutcheson onwards. "Love
and compassion", Adam Ferguson wrote in his *Essay*, "are

the most powerful principles in the human breast."[21] Galt
was too honest a realist not to temper the benevolence with
self-interest, greed, malice and envy, but his characters
and, no doubt Galt himself, predominantly agreed with
Mrs Soorocks, "It is our duty to help ane anither in this
howling wilderness".[22]

REFERENCES

1. L.L., Vol. I, p. 270.
2. Gordon, p. 129.
3. Las., Chapt. XVI, p. 67.
4. Las., Chapt. V, p. 22.
5. D. M. Moir: *Biographical Memoir*, p. XI.
6. Oliphant: Vol. I, pp. 460–1.
7. Las., Chapt. XIV, p. 59.
8. Las., Chapt. X, p. 43.
9. L.L., Vol. I, p. 271.
10. Galt in a letter to William Blackwood, quoted by Ian A. Gordon in
    Introduction to his edition—p. ix.
11. Las., Chapt. I, p. 2.
12. Las., Chapt. II, p. 7.
13. Las., Chapt. XXXVII, p. 163.
14. Las. Chapt. II, p. 9.
15. Sir George Douglas: *The Blackwood Group*—Famous Scots Series
    (1897), pp. 72–3.
16. B. A. Booth: Introduction to his edition of *The Gathering of the West*
    (1939), p. 21.
17. Ian Jack: *Oxford History of English Literature*, Vol. X (1963), p. 234.
18. Walter Allen: *The English Novel*—Pelican Edition (1973), p. 129.
19. Jane Helen Findlater: *Stones from a Glass House* (1904), pp. 95–6.
20. Ruth I. Aldrich: *John Galt* (1978), p. 93.
21. Ferguson: p. 36.
22. Las., Chapt. XII, p. 53.

CHAPTER VIII

RINGAN GILHAIZE (1823)

Throughout Galt's novels there are many allusions to Walter Scott. Dr Pringle and Mr Snodgrass are discovered reading one of the Waverley Novels. Galt has characters and episodes, like Mrs Eadie in *The Entail* or the gipsies in *Sir Andrew Wylie* who seem to have been suggested by Scott. Sir Walter himself appears in *The Steamboat* and *The Gathering of the West*. In *The Spae Wife* and *Rothelan*, Galt attempted, unsuccessfully, historical novels in the Scott manner. Up to this point, however, Scott's influence on Galt had been slight and more deleterious than beneficial. The distinctive strengths of the two men lay in opposite directions, although sometimes their worlds coincided as in the characters of Provost Pawkie and Bailie Nicol Jarvie. Scott's celebrated comment on Jane Austen might be applied also to Galt:

> That young lady had a talent for describing the involvements and feelings and characters of ordinary life, which is to me the most wonderful I ever met with. The Big Bow-wow strain I can do myself like any now going; but the exquisite touch, which renders ordinary commonplace things and characters interesting, from the truth of the description and the sentiment, is denied to me.[1]

Galt generally did not have the Big Bow-wow strain either, but he did have the exquisite touch.

With *Ringan Gilhaize*, the relation between the two writers took a new turn. Galt was infuriated by Scott's handling of the Covenanters in *Old Mortality* and reacted against it so strongly that it led him to write a book that was not only different in kind from anything that he had done before but from anything written by anyone else. He was right to claim that it was unique.[2] It was a historical novel certainly. It was also another of Galt's imaginary autobiographies. Its uniqueness lay in the fusion of these two techniques to convey a convincing account of a long, complex and controversial period of history through the eyes of a participant who was actively and passionately involved.

In his *Literary Life*, Galt gave his own explanation of his motives in writing *Ringan Gilhaize*:

> . . . The book itself was certainly suggested by Sir Walter Scott's *Old Mortality*, in which I thought he treated the defenders of the Presbyterian Church with too much levity, and not according to my impressions derived from the history of that time. Indeed, to tell the truth, I was hugely provoked that he, the descendant of Scott of Harden, who was fined in those days forty thousand pounds Scots for being a Presbyterian, or rather for countenancing his lady for being so, should have been so forgetful of what was due to the spirit of that epoch, as to throw it into what I felt was ridicule.
>
> The fact is, that I am not myself quite a disinterested person on the subject of the Covenant, though, God knows, I have no pretension to the purity it implied in the conduct of those who signed it. A collateral ancestor of mine, namely John Galt of Gateside, was banished, in 1684, to Carolina, for refusing to call the affair of Bothwell Bridge a rebellion, and to renounce the Covenant.[3]

Galt was not alone in resenting Scott's treatment of the Covenanters in *Old Mortality*. As soon as the book appeared in December 1816, Dr Thomas McCrie, the biographer of John Knox, launched the controversy with a series of

articles in the *Edinburgh Christian Instructor*, roundly
accusing Scott of misrepresenting history. James Hogg's
novel about the persecution of the Covenanters, *The
Brownie of Bodsbeck*, was published in 1818 and read like
another reply to Scott, although Hogg said that he had
written it before the publication of *Old Mortality*. For
McCrie, Hogg and Galt, and indeed probably most people
in Scotland at the time, the Covenanters were national
heroes who had made a heroic stand for their religious
beliefs. On the other side, the Royalists had broken solemn
undertakings and launched an unprovoked and brutal
campaign against them. It was not a matter of argument
over points of historical detail, but of deeply felt conviction.
In John Buchan's words, "The Covenanters had become to
the majority of the people of Scotland a race of demigods
and saints, and their story had been written even by
sophisticated Edinburgh lawyers, in a vein of hagio-
graphy".[4] Scott had offended these feelings by appearing
to ridicule the Covenanters and to present Claverhouse in
too favourable a light. As Galt makes one of his characters
in *The Steamboat* say, Scott "had laid an irreverant hand on
the ark of our great national cause, the Covenant".[5]

There is a sense, too, as that phrase "national cause"
suggests, in which the Covenanters had become a symbol
of a struggle over not only points of religious doctrine but of
a wider struggle for the freedom of Scotland or for freedom
itself. Scott recognised this in making Henry Morton say to
Claverhouse: "I am willing you should be aware that there
are yet Scotsmen who can assert the liberties of Scotland".[6]
Galt is even more explicit. Ringan Gilhaize quotes from
the Declaration of Arbroath: " 'It is not for glory', we said
in the words of those brave Scottish barons that redeemed,
with King Robert the Bruce, their native land from the
thraldom of the English Edward, 'nor is it for riches,
neither is it for honour, but it is for liberty alone we
contend, which no true man will lose but with his life' ".[7]
To drive the point home, Galt prints the whole text of the

Declaration in an appendix to the novel. This extension of the significance of the Covenanting struggle is not unreasonable. The Covenanters were resisting attempts at interference with the Scottish church imposed from the outside by absentee Kings resting on English power. There was therefore an analogy with Edward I's invasions.

In addition, Galt widens the theme to the justification of the general right of resistance to unjust authority. He establishes this in the first paragraph of the book, when Ringan speaks of what his grandfather had told him of the struggles of the Reformation:

> For my father's father was out in the raids of that tempestuous season, and it was by him, and from the stories he was wont to tell of what the government did, when drunken with the sorceries of the gorgeous Roman harlot, and rampaging with the wrath of Moloch and of Belial, it trampled on the hearts and thought to devour the souls of the subjects, that I first was taught to feel, know, and understand, the divine right of resistance.

Since the Covenanters were poor and humble and their oppressors aristocratic, there is also an element of class conflict. Although the issues in *Ringan Gilhaize* turn on questions of religion, it is also a book with strong political implications.

Ringan Gilhaize was not the first of Galt's novels to speak of the "divine right of resistance". In the introductory chapter of the *Annals of the Parish*, Mr Balwhidder gives us the text of his last sermon, preached "on the last Sabbath of the year 1810". In the course of it, he refers to the time when "the banner of the oppressor was planted of old, and the war-horse trampled in the blood of the martyrs". He means, of course, the Covenanters, and he continues:

> I do not counsel passive obedience; that is a doctrine that the Church of Scotland can never abide; but the

> divine right of resistance, which, in the days of her
> trouble, she so bravely asserted against popish and
> prelatic usurpations, was never resorted to till the
> attempt was made to remove the ark of the tabernacle
> from her.[9]

That is the authentic voice of the Covenant or of
Ringan himself. Mr Balwhidder in 1810, having lived
through the age of the Enlightenment, is recalling the
sentiments and using the language of the Covenanters,
even when he is preaching Christian resignation. This is
not an anachronism. Along with the other intellectual
influences of the time, the traditions of the Covenanters
and their biblical vocabulary were alive in oral traditions
and in the pulpit of the Kirk. All of the ministers in Galt's
novels reflect it in their more impassioned moments. Both
Hogg and Galt appealed to oral tradition as well as written
records in claiming that *Old Mortality* was a distortion of
the facts. Galt himself was obviously brought up in the
tradition—"I am not myself quite a disinterested person
on the subject of the Covenant"—and he had absorbed
covenanting literature to the point where he could write
the language with the fluency and conviction of a mother
tongue.

Neither Scott nor Galt were religious bigots or even of
any strong religious conviction at all. Both were essentially
products of the Scottish Enlightenment, sceptical, opposed
to fanaticism, and approving moderation and good sense.
In their novels on the Covenanters, neither took a
completely black and white view and both were prepared
to see merits on both sides. Scott conceded the brutality of
the Royalists and some of his Covenanters rise to heights of
heroism as others sink into fanaticism and absurdity. His
hero, Henry Morton, is the moderate man in the middle
and he after all allies himself with the Covenanting cause.
Galt, consistently with his optimistic and Enlightenment
view of the benevolence of human nature, shows instances

of generosity and compassion even among the oppressors. More than once, Ringan is helped by a kindly gaoler. Nor does Galt play down the excesses of the Reformers in the sacking and "demolishment" of the religious houses.

Even with their fair-mindedness and tolerance, both Galt and Scott confessed to prejudices on this particular question. Galt declared his family tradition in the *Literary Life*. I would not go myself as far as John MacQueen who says boldly "Galt himself remained a Calvinist to the end of his days".[8] It seems to me from the evidence of his writing that Galt was predominantly a sceptic in the Enlightenment tradition, but one tinged with his Presbyterian upbringing, like so many other people in Scotland then and since. The prejudices of Walter Scott, on the other hand, were in the opposite direction. As he recalls in the Ashestiel memoir, family influence in his case was strongly towards Jacobitism. Lockhart tells us that the only picture which Scott had in his study was a portrait of Claverhouse and that he defended him as "every inch a soldier and a gentleman".[9]

Claverhouse plays an important part in both *Old Mortality* and *Ringan Gilhaize*. For Ringan, he becomes the embodiment of the forces of oppression and the novel ends with his death at the hands of Ringan himself at the Battle of Killiecrankie. Galt, no doubt, aims directly at Scott when he makes Ringan comment: "the implacable rage with which Claverhouse persecuted the Covenanters has been extenuated by some discreet historians, on the plea of his being an honourable officer deduced from his soldiery worth elsewhere, whereas the truth is, that his cruelties in the shire of Ayr, and other of our western parts, were less the fruit of his instructions, wide and severe as they were, than of his own mortified vanity and malignant revenge".[10] Later, Ringan learns that his son's head "was cut off and sent in ignomy to Edinburgh . . . by the command of Claverhouse himself".[11] Different interpretations of the character and behaviour of Claverhouse were however not the main point at issue. In his explanation of the origins of the book, Galt does not mention Claverhouse at all. He was taking issue with Scott not over his handling of the Royalists but of the Covenanters. His charge was that Scott had treated them with "too much levity" and exposed them to ridicule. I think that it is true that however fair Scott tried to be to both sides, the overall impression which *Old Mortality* leaves with the reader is that the Covenanters were ridiculous, when they were not dangerous fanatics. Galt's objectives were to restore to the Covenanters the dignity and seriousness of which *Old Mortality* had deprived them and to explain and justify the fanaticism into which they had been driven by persecution.

In giving impressions of the Covenanters so widely opposed to one another, both Scott and Galt rely partly on their use of language derived from the historical and literary records. Biblical phraseology rose readily to the lips of the Covenanters. At its best, this could rise to eloquence or at least convey a feeling of solemnity and seriousness. At its worst, it could use the Old Testament to produce a hideously inflated language of violence, or become ridiculous when it was applied to comically inappropriate subjects. Scott emphasises both of these; the violent, for instance in the words of Habbakuk Mucklewrath:

> Who talks of peace and safe conduct? who speaks of mercy to the bloody house of the malignants? I say take the infants and dash them against the stones; take the daughters and the mothers of the house and hurl them from the battlements of their trust, that the dogs may fatten on their blood as they did on that of Jezabel, the spouse of Ahab, and that their carcasses may be dung to the face of the field even in the portion of their fathers![12]

or the comic from Mause Headrigg:

Only just thus far, my leddy, . . . that prelacy is like
the great golden image in the plain of Dura, and that
as Shadrach, Meshach, and Abednego, were borne
out in refusing to bow down and worship, so neither
shall Cuddy Headrigg, your leddyship's poor pleugh-
man, at least wi' his auld mither's consent, make
murgeons or Jenny-flections, as they ca' them, in the
house of the prelates and curates, nor gird him wi'
armour to fight in their cause, either at the sound of
kettle-drums, organs, bagpipes, or any other kind of
music whatever.[13]

Galt, with at least equal fidelity to his sources, maintains
a level of plain but dignified diction, which can touch
eloquence at important moments. Here, for instance, is
Ringan at the climax of the book after his shooting of
Claverhouse:

In the same moment I looked up, and there was a
vision in the air as if all the angels of brightness, and
the martyrs in their vestments of glory, were as-
sembled on the walls and battlements of heaven to
witness the event—and I started up and cried, "I
have delivered my native land!" But in the same
instant I remembered to whom the glory was due, and
falling again on my knees, I raised my hands and
bowed my head as I said, "Not mine, O Lord, but
thine is the victory!"[14]

Scott, in a third-person narrative, had to introduce
Covenanting speech only in the conversations. Galt by
making Ringan tell his story in the first person had to maintain it throughout. The extravagances of Mucklewrath
would have been intolerable at such length, as well as an
unfair historical misrepresentation. Galt's more restrained
idiom is not only a plausible interpretation of the way in
which a Covenanter might have written (as may be
verified by comparing it with the originals in Robert

Wodrow's four volumes of *The History of the Suffering of the Church of Scotland*), but he also made it a flexible instrument of fluent narrative prose. This was an impressive feat of historical re-creation and stylistic virtuosity.

But if Galt was to make a case for the Covenanters he had to do much more than restore the dignity of their speech. He evidently felt that he had to take the history back to the Reformation. Ringan says in the opening paragraph: "I intend mainly to bear witness to these passages of the late bloody persecution in which I was myself both a soldier and a sufferer", but adds: "At the same time it is needful that I should rehearse as much of what happened in the troubles of the Reformation, as, in its effects and influences, worked upon the issues of my own life". In fact, the earlier period in the lifetime of Ringan's grandfather takes up about half of the whole book. Galt evidently wanted to show that the Covenanters saw themselves as defending the purity of the Church of the Reformation and as continuing the same struggle and exercising the same "divine right of resistance". Galt hoped to strengthen the case for the Covenanters by presenting their historical credentials.

Since Galt had chosen to write the book in his more successful style, the first-person narrative, the extension of time presented him with an awkward problem. The period he had to cover spanned about three lifetimes, the 150 years or so from the beginning of the Reformation in Scotland in the 1550s to the death of Claverhouse at Killiecrankie in 1680. As William Roughead says, the time covered equals that of three of the Waverley Novels, *The Monastery*, *The Abbot* and *Old Mortality*.[15] How was this to be accomplished by one personal narrator? Galt hit upon a somewhat implausible device. The whole book is told in the voice of Ringan Gilhaize whose personal experiences occupy the second half. For the earlier period Ringan retells the reminiscences of his grandfather. Even so, to get the necessary time-span, Galt has to ask the reader to believe that the grandfather lived to the age of 91 and was able to pass on a detailed oral account of his life to Ringan who was only eight at the time of his death.[16]

Galt could, of course, have avoided this difficulty giving us two successive but distinctive narratives, one of the grandfather and the other by the grandson. In fact the book does read like that because the earlier part is necessarily in the third person. There is a passage in the *Literary Life* where Galt argues that he had a deliberate purpose in relaying the whole story through the filter, as it were, of the mind of Ringan:

> I have supposed a Covenanter relating the adventures of his grandfather who lived during the Reformation. It was therefore necessary that I should conceive distinctly what a Covenanter would think of a Reformer in the church, to enable him to relate what such a person would do in the time of John Knox. There was here, if I may be allowed the expression, a transfusion of character that could only be rightly understood by showing how a Reformer himself acted and felt in the opinion of a Covenanter. To enable the reader to estimate the invention put forth in the work, and to judge of the manner in which the Covenanter performed his task, I made him give his autobiography, in which was kept out of view every thing that might recall the separate existence of John Galt.[16]

This is a very subtle notion, and a new experiment in narrative technique. What Galt appears to be saying is that he intended in the first part of the book not merely to give us account of the events of the Reformation but to add the extra dimension of the Covenanter's view of these events. Indeed the first sentence of the book sets the tone: "It is a thing past all contesting, that, in the Reformation, there was a spirit of far greater carnality among the champions of the cause, than among those who in later times so courageously, under the Lord, upheld the unspotted banner of the Covenant".

Galt was working in two historical planes simultaneously and was doing this to show that the Covenanters not only carried on the struggle of the Reformers but did so in a purer spirit. As Ringan goes on to say, there was a "spiritual and hallowed difference". This was such a bold narrative device that it is perhaps not surprising that it was not generally appreciated. As Galt adds at the end of the passage which I have just quoted from the *Literary Life*: "I cannot have succeeded in my object; not one person has ever evinced an apprehension of the intention which I thought would have attracted consideration, and yet I do not see myself that I have failed in my object".

The first half of the book is only preparation for the main theme, the persecution of the Covenanters and the effects which this had on them. In a sense, this is a detailed study of a process which Scott in *Old Mortality* resumes in a sentence:

> It is Habbakuk Mucklewrath ... whom the enemy have long detained in captivity in forts and castles, until his understanding hath departed from him, and as I fear, an evil demon hath possessed him.[17]

We see Mucklewrath only in his madness when he looked "more like the resurrection of some cannibal priest, or druid red from his human sacrifice, than like an earthly mortal". Ringan Gilhaize, too, is driven to madness, when he describes himself as "an infirm grey-haired man, with a deranged head and a broken heart". He has a period of "eclipse",[18] when he is not conscious of what is going on around him. He, too, is driven to violence and fanaticism to the point where he kills Claverhouse in a spirit of religious ecstasy. But, unlike Mucklewrath, he remains throughout a credible, suffering, even kindly human being on whom even his gaolers take pity. Our sympathies have been enlisted because we see him from the beginning as he is gradually transformed by the cruelties inflicted on him and his family. For long, Ringan is generous to his enemies and reluctant to seek revenge. The turning point comes when he is released from prison and returns home with his son to find that his wife and daughters have been killed. On the road, they encounter a party of dragoons. Even at this point, with every reason to fear the worst, Ringan clings to his charitable instinct:

> "I wonder", said my son, "that they did na speak to me: I thought they had a black look."
>
> "No doubt, Joseph," was my answer, "the men are no lost to a' sense of shame. They canna but be rebuked at the sight of a man that, maybe against their will, poor fellows, they were sent to oppress."
>
> "I dinna like them the day, father, they're unco like ill-doers", said the thoughtful and observing stripling.
>
> But my spirit was at the time full of good-will towards all men, and I reasoned with him against giving way to unkind thoughts, expunding, to the best of my ability, the nature of gospel-charity, and the heavenlyness of good-will.[19]

The novel has become a study of the process, unhappily more familiar to us than to Galt's contemporaries, of the way violence breeds violence, and how a sincere, pious and kind man can be driven by persecution to fanaticism. It is a grim and sombre theme. From its nature, and the character of his chosen narrator, Galt denied himself his usual resources of comedy and irony. Inevitably, it has to stay on a constant note, with only the slightest concessions to light relief. It makes up for this by the power and realism of its scenes of violence and desolation and by the study of human reactions under extreme pressure.

Although the atmosphere of *Ringan Gilhaize* is very different from the "Tales of the West", there is a historical continuity between them, as Mr Balwhidder made explicit in his last sermon. The subsequent evolution of the society which was the subject of the Tales was deeply influenced by the Reformation and the struggle of the Covenant. Galt emphasised this by placing the same part of the West of Scotland at the heart of the action in *Ringan Gilhaize*. The Grandfather was born in Linlithgow and travelled widely over Central Scotland in the service of the Reformers, but he finally settled down at Quharist on the river Garnock close to the "godly town of Irvine".[20] The land was given to him by Lord Eglinton, an ancestor of the Lord Eaglsham of the *Annals* or *The Provost*. Ringan only leaves the area when the fortunes of war demand. We have moved back in time but we are still in the same place. *Ringan Gilhaize* gives an added depth to the "Tales of the West" by suggesting the historical roots of the attitudes and assumptions prevalent a hundred years or so later on; the egalitarianism, the distrust of hierarchy and ostentation, the resilience of people accustomed to hardship, and the community spirit derived from a common struggle. They were the qualities which made the Age of Improvement possible and which were transformed by it. There is a sense in which *Ringan Gilhaize* is the necessary introduction to the *Annals of the Parish*. Together the two books could be read as a commentary in advance on Max Weber's theory on the Protestant ethic and the spirit of Capitalism.

Ringan Gilhaize is a novel without any of the ingredients of easy popularity. It also took sides in a way that was unfashionable with the novel readers of the time. Galt, as George Kitchin says, "had taken his stand with the humble and persecuted". He had "failed to realise that if he was going to get on with the literary Tories he would have to sit quiet when Sir Walter dealt all too faithfully with the Covenanters in *Old Mortality*. That is just what he could not do."[21] At the time when they were preoccupied with Jacobin sentiments among discontented weavers and the pressures for parliamentary reform, the literary Tories had little sympathy with the humble and persecuted. The literary Whigs were equally averse to the language and sentiments of religious enthusiasm. It is therefore not surprising that the novel was unsuccessful on its first publication, and had neither favourable notice in the reviews nor the rapid reprinting to which Galt had grown accustomed. In the *Edinburgh Review*, Francis Jeffrey conceded that the novel had "some animated and poetical descriptions" and episodes of "considerable power and effect"; but his conclusion was damning:

> But still the book is tiresome, and without effect. The narrative is neither pleasing nor probable, and the calamities are too numerous, and too much alike; and the uniformity of the tone of actual suffering and dim religious hope, weighs like a load on the spirit of the reader. There is no interesting complication of events or adventure, and no animating development or catastrophe.[22]

It seems to me that Jeffrey was condemning *Ringan Gilhaize* for not being a novel of a different kind and that he failed to recognise Galt's success in achieving what he set out to do.

Galt himself was convinced that *Ringan Gilhaize* was his finest work and that posterity would see its merits.[23] Indeed in 1897, Sir George Douglas at last did so when he wrote in his book *The Blackwood Group*:

> And into the spirit of the particular movement with which he deals, it must be acknowledged that Galt has penetrated further than Scott. For the true aim of the writer of a novel treating of these times in Scotland was obviously to disregard such a non-essential as sporadic insincerity, to penetrate the outer crust of dourness and intolerance, and whilst maintaining the balance of perfect fairness, to compel the reader to sympathise with the best of the Covenanters, not only in their bitter resentment of cruel wrongs, but in their most earnestly cherished and loftiest ideals. And this,

which Scott did not care to do, Galt has accomplished, in virtue of which achievement his book is entitled to rank as the epic of the Scottish religious wars.[24]

And this is not the whole force of the book. Apart from re-creating the events of the Reformation and the religious wars as they might have appeared to a participant, Galt had written a book which is distressingly relevant to the present age in its analysis of the nature and effects of political and religious violence.

REFERENCES

1. Sir Walter Scott: *Journal*, Entry for 14 March 1826.
2. Aur., Vol. II, p. 220.
3. L.L., Vol. I, p. 254.
4. John Buchan: *The Life of Sir Walter Scott* (edition of 1961), p. 160.
5. Sb., Chapt. XIV.
6. Sir Walter Scott: *Old Mortality*, Chapt. XIII.
7. R.G., Chapt. XXVI.
8. John MacQueen in *John Galt 1779–1979* (edited by C. A. Whatley, 1978), p. 108.
9. J. G. Lockhart: *Memoirs of Sir Walter Scott* (edition 1900), Chapt. XXXVII, Vol. III, p. 86.
10. R.G., Chapt. XXVI.
11. R.G., Chapt. XXXIX.
12. Sir Walter Scott: *Old Mortality*, Chapt. XXII.
13. *Ibid.*, Chapt. VII.
14. R.G., Chapt. XCIII.
15. William Roughead: Introduction to 1936 edition of R.G., p. vii.
16. L.L., Vol. I, p. 250.
17. Sir Walter Scott: *Old Mortality*, Chapt. XXII.
18. R.G., Chapt. LXXVIII.
19. R.G., Chapt. LXXV.
20. R.G., Chapt. XXXVII.
21. George Kitchin in *Edinburgh Essays on Scots Literature* (1933), p. 122.
22. Jeffrey: Vol. III, pp. 518–19.
23. L.L., Vol. I, p. 258 (quoted above at end of Chapt. I).
24. Sir George Douglas: *The Blackwood Group* (1897), p. 73.

CHAPTER IX

THE NORTH AMERICAN AND
THE POLITICAL NOVELS

Lawrie Todd or the Settlers in the Woods (1830)

In 1830, when his affairs were at low ebb and he was pressed for money, Galt accepted an offer of an advance of £300 for a three-volume novel. The result was *Lawrie Todd*, an imaginary autobiography of a Scottish settler in the United States. It was not entirely imaginary, because the early part of the novel followed the memoirs of Grant Thorburn, a seed merchant in New York. This takes less than a quarter of the whole book or less than two of the nine parts into which it is divided. For the rest, the imaginary narrator takes over, moving from New York to the Genesee country west of Utica, then the frontier of the new expanding state. Galt was therefore experimenting with yet another new variation to his familiar form of imaginary autobiography, by projecting a given and real life character into an imagined series of events which went far beyond his actual experience. Galt's version can readily be compared with Thorburn's text because it was published in 1834 as *Forty Years' Residence in America, or The Doctrine of a Particular Providence*, with an introduction by Galt himself.

In his *Literary Life*, Galt said of *Lawrie Todd* that it was first of a new series of books in which "the disposition to be didactic was more indulged than I previously thought could be rendered consistent with a regular story". The didactic intention is not intrusive, and in fact Galt admitted that most of his readers had taken the book as a novel meant only for entertainment.[1] By didactic, in this case, he seems to have in mind only the usefulness to future settlers of an accurate account of conditions on the frontier. He was aiming at realism. "I am not aware that any book existed prior to that publication which gave a first account of backwood operations, at least these operations which it was my duty to study, and of which an authentic account could not but lessen many of the privations and hardships of settling. . . . I say this with a perfect recollection of Mr Cooper's descriptions applicable to settlers, which are as little like reality as his sea pictures are inimitable."[2]

Galt was, of course, drawing on his Canadian experience, where he had been in charge of precisely the same sort of undertaking, clearing and settling virgin forest. "I did not go about with my eyes shut either with respect to the character of settlers, or of colonial operations, under my particular charge."[3] There must have been many similarities between Canadian and American experience in face of the same physical challenge. At the same time, Galt was conscious of different attitudes in the two countries, as he subsequently made explicit in *Bogle Corbet*. In *Lawrie Todd*, the whole atmosphere is distinctly American: restless, ambitious, expansive, egalitarian and conducive to successful capitalist speculation. Shortly after his arrival in New York, Lawrie Todd prays and then remarks (foreshadowing Max Weber): "I rose from my kneeling, refreshed in body and mind, and went forth to earn my first cent in America".[4] He consistently advocates adaptation to American ways: "You will neither find comfort nor increase here, unless you conform, not only to the customs of those among whom your lot has been cast, but to their opinions and ways of thinking. The people on this side of the Atlantic have no ancestors."[5]

Lawrie Todd, shrewd, sensible, thoughtful, honest and hard-working, as well as adaptable, is clearly likely to succeed. And succeed he does, acquiring both wealth and the respect of the community. In a note at the end of the second edition (1833), Galt compares Lawrie Todd to Sir

Andrew Wylie: "In writing Sir Andrew Wylie, I was led by the opinion of a friend ... to make it more of a common novel than was intended. I wished to show a friendless Scotchman rising by the force of his own abilities into opulence and consideration; but I was induced to give him a patron. In this work I have reverted to my original plan, and my endeavours to represent unassisted merit have not been a failure." Yet, in the very last sentence of the book, Galt makes Lawrie say that the story of his life "serves to show how little of good fortune is owing to our own foresight". This may reflect Grant Thorburn's views on Particular Providence which attributes all to the will of God; but, as with Mr Balwhidder, it comes close in the final analysis to Adam Ferguson's view of the way in which society evolves independently of human intention.

One of the first reviews of the book, in the *Literary Gazette* of 30 January 1830, said that Galt had "that peculiar talent which, to this day, makes Robinson Crusoe and his lonely island a thing of tangible memory and actual existence". Galt was gratified by the comparison and suggested that he had made similar use of Thorburn's account as Defoe did of Andrew Selkirk's.[6] As Ian Gordon remarks, there are indeed scenes in Lawrie Todd which "have the sharp brilliance of Defoe".[7] At the same time this comparison, and the alternative title, *The Settlers in the Woods*, give a false impression. There are several chapters in Part III of the novel when Lawrie and his family first move into the woods where he has to contend with raw nature, with snakes, wolves, bears and forest fires. But Lawrie is not on a "lonely island"; he is never alone. He is not struggling to achieve isolated survival, but to develop a community. Towns are founded. Lawrie identifies, and helps to satisfy, the social needs for a church, a school and magistrates. Banks, a newspaper, industries and hotels follow. Judiville, the town founded by Lawrie, grows in a few years from nothing to a population of 7,000 with 6 churches and a theatre. In fact *Lawrie Todd* for a different society in a different stage of development, is performing for early 19th-century America the same function as *Annals of the Parish* for 18th-century Scotland. It is an accurate, if "theoretical", social history of a society in a phase of radical and rapid change. *Lawrie Todd* does not have the economy, or the irony and humour of the earlier book (except here and there), but it has similar qualities of realism and of intelligent understanding of a historical process.

Lawrie Todd, unlike Galt's other narrators, comes not from the West of Scotland, but from the east, "Bonnytown", a village close to Dalkeith and therefore near Edinburgh. When he returns to Scotland for a visit of about a year, he spends most of his time again in the east, at "Chucky Stanes" on the Tweed, which Galt in a note tells us is Peebles. For this reason, if he was not also restrained by his English publisher, Galt is denied the full canon of his Ayrshire Scots; he makes Lawrie write a simple, lucid prose, invigorated by effective use of a good vocabulary of Scots words and phrases. One of the more deplorable, and amusing characters, Bailie Waft, is from the West, and his speech reflects it. As a prolonged east-west joke, he constantly uses his western gift of the gab to outsmart the more honest and straightforward, but less quick-witted, easterner. Galt also indulges in some of his teasing of the towns on the Clyde. Mr Semple from Renfrewshire, for instance, proposes that a church to be built at Judiville should be modelled on "a new church at Greenock, one of the finest buildings in Christendom; at least, so said Mr Semple, and he but repeated the opinion of all the inhabitants of Greenock, the most enlightened community in the West of Scotland, scarcely excepting even that of Port Glasgow—so justly, for its taste in the fine arts, denominated the Florence of the West".[8]

There is, of course, not only Scottish speech in the novel, but American as well. This is especially displayed in the most developed of the American characters, Mr Hoskins, taciturn but kind and shrewd, and tirelessly alert for a profitable speculation. Galt's glossary contains Yankee as well as Scottish words. Many of the former are now commonplace—"Boss: an overseer of mechanics; Help: a domestic female servant"—but this must be one of their first appearances in print.

Galt gives free rein to his comic impulses only when Lawrie returns on his visit to Scotland. The whole episode, particularly the scenes in Chucky Stanes in Part VII, could be extracted to form a novella on their own. Indeed their atmosphere is quite distinct from the rest of the novel, and not unlike the *Last of the Lairds* in tone. The action revolves around the absurd figure of the perjinct and predatory Miss Benney Needles—who "prided herself on being one of the best interpreters of the Scotch novels"[10]—and her efforts to entice Lawrie into marriage. This is outrageous knock-about comedy, reminiscent of Smollett, to whom Galt in fact makes a reference.[10] Galt seems to be able to indulge in this sort of thing only on his native heath.

Unlike his model, Grant Thorburn, Lawrie eventually decides to leave America and return home for good. He is forced into a struggle of conscience when he is pressed to stand for Congress and he realises that this would involve a change of citizenship. He decides that "truly it is an awful thing for a man to forswear his native land", and reflects in a passage reminiscent of Ringan Gilhaize and his association of the Covenanters with the heroic figures of the Scottish War of Independence:

> My conscience could not away with the thought of renouncing the right to claim paternity with Sir William Wallace and the brave old bald-headed worthies of the Covenant, my father's household gods, on whose altar, our lowly hearth, the incense of a special thanksgiving was every Sabbath evening offered to Heaven, for having sent them to redeem

and sanctify "our ancient and never-conquered Kingdom of Scotland" [11]

The religious tone of this passage is not typical of Lawrie's account. Grant Thorburn, as is obvious even from his title page, was strongly religious. Galt reflects this in the early chapters which follow Thorburn, but it becomes much less apparent as Lawrie becomes preoccupied with the practical problems of carving a society out of the virgin forest. He is not above making money out of the construction of the first church, "It was a profitable, but not a fortune-making job".[12] When it is built it is leased not to the Presbyterians, as he would have preferred, but to the Methodists, who have more money. Lawrie justifies this to himself in a passage worthy of Mr Pawkie: "I had lived long enough in the world to discern that there is little use in raising an opposition, unless there be some chance of accomplishing the intent of it. In this there was none; the question was between God and Mammon, and the majority of the shareholders were zealous to make money."[13]

This episode of the disposal of the new church is one of the ways in which Lawrie falls foul of the stickit minister, Amos Bell, the most complex piece of psychological analysis in the book. Mr Bell, sorely tried by a series of disappointments and a disastrous marriage, declines into a murderous insanity directed against the inoffensive Lawrie, a contributory cause of his decision to leave America.

Lawrie Todd was well received when it first appeared. The reviewers in *Fraser's Magazine*, for instance, thought that it was one of Galt's best novels, "for it has all the pleasing qualities which the public so well recognised in the *Annals of the Parish*, spread over a much larger surface, and applied to objects of far higher general interest".[14] As late as 1888, the *Chambers's Cyclopaedia of English Literature* said that *Lawrie Todd* was the equal of *Annals of the*

Parish or *The Entail*.[15] These are views which few people would now share. *Lawrie Todd* does not have the ironic subtlety of the *Annals* or the emotional depth or linguistic virtuosity of *The Entail*. Still, it is an interesting novel which does not deserve its present neglect. In the 19th century, there were at least four British editions and no less than sixteen in the United States, but it seems that there have been none in this century. It is long overdue for reprinting.

Bogle Corbet (1831)

Of the second three-volume novel which he wrote for Colburn and Bentley, Galt said in the *Literary Life*: "My publisher suggested Bogle Corbet to me; but although a tolerable book, it is another proof, if one were wanting, that booksellers step from their line when they give orders, like to an upholsterer for a piece of furniture ... to write three volumes at the request of another, in a satisfactory manner, and without an occasional sense of drudgery, is beyond my power".[16]

In the Preface to the book itself, he tells us, somewhat discouragingly for an introduction to a novel: "The Author had proposed to offer the result of his observations in a regularly didactic form, but upon reflection, a theoretic biography seemed better calculated to ensure the effect desired". He explains these didactic purposes in his *Autobiography*.[17] His idea was to provide a guide book to Canada, particularly for a new "genteeler class" of emigrants, those of some education who relied more on their brains and capital than on their hands to make their way in the New World. In addition, he wanted to explain the causes which had motivated this new class of emigrants, to examine the effects of the introduction of cotton manufacture into Scotland, and, for good measure or to help to fill the three volumes, to describe the situation of the slaves in the West Indies (of which he knew nothing at first hand). It sounds an unlikely formula for a novel.

And yet, the result, as Galt says, was a "tolerable book".

He is often his own most discerning critic and he makes a real point when he goes on to say:

> I had models for the principal characters in my eye, and in few have I been so uniformly successful in the portraiture. The persons in my view have been delineated with considerable truth, but not always, I suspect, with that sort of felicity, which is necessary to render a book agreeable to the general reader.[18]

It is possible to believe that the characters in *Bogle Corbet* are indeed a faithful rendering of Galt's models, but the portraits are only skin deep and leave little distinct impression on the mind. It seems that Galt's sense of comedy and his psychological insight both desert him when he writes in English instead of Scots. Bogle Corbet is Scottish and so are a number of the other characters. But for the most part, the narrator and the rest speak a flat and fushionless English. It seems that Galt's distinctive qualities depend on the use of Scots, and that he could not express them in any other way. The point which Galt had made in his *Biographical Sketch of John Wilson* at the beginning of his literary career applied to his own writing: it was in Scots that "he expresses himself with most ease and vivacity" and when he used English "he uses a species of translation, which checks the versatility of fancy, and restrains the genuine and spontaneous flow of his conceptions".[19] How much have we lost, one wonders, by the pressures on Scottish writers, through the force of the educational system, social convention and the demands of the English market, to make them abandon their native speech and write in English?

The interest of *Bogle Corbet* does not lie in character or incident but in social comment. It covers a wide range. The narrator, Bogle Corbet himself, is an orphan, born in the West Isles about 1780, but brought up near Glasgow. His curators, or guardians, decide to place him in a commercial career in the cotton industry. For a time he works in a cotton mill in Glasgow where the workers are much influenced by French Revolutionary thought. He goes into partnership which fails because of the ineptitude of his partner, while Bogle himself is representing the firm in London. The creditors send him to Jamaica to dispose of the stock. He returns and sets up as a merchant in the West Indian trade. Business declines and he finds his income inadequate for the needs of his growing family. He flirts with the idea of writing for money, but finally decides to emigrate to Canada. The last volume of the novel is an account of the conditions he found there and his efforts to build up a new life.

Galt was particularly pleased with the accuracy of his account of Canada: "Canada, indeed, must have altered rapidly if Bogle Corbet be not a true guide to settlers of his rank", he said in the *Autobiography*.[20] Even the "view of the West Indian society, though it is altogether a combination of the fancy it is done with solicitude and care".[21] The account of commercial life in Glasgow and London comes from first hand experience. Very often, in fact, Bogle seems to be speaking for Galt himself at this particularly depressing ebb in his fortunes. "I think the first few months after the publication of Bogle Corbet were the most unacceptable of my whole life, always excepting the early period of my residence in London", he remarked in the *Literary Life*.[22] Bogle is disillusioned with commerce; he is "tramelled with a natural ineptitude to trade",[23] also with London, "the crowd that fills the streets is more friendless than the sands of the Arabian desert".[24] He is discouraged by what he hears of literary life: "Nothing is so easy as to find fault; and hence it is, that the greatest fault-finders are the weakest of men.—The rule applies to critics."[25] "A merchant may be permitted to write a pamphlet, but for a man who has been bred to commerce of any kind to attempt more, is high treason in the republic of letters."[26] ... "I might try my hand at something like a work on political economy; a cosy inborn science, on which those who understand it least are commonly the most fluent writers."[27] On the short visit to the Highlands, Bogle discovers a ruined society in the aftermath of the '45 and the Clearances, "This country is now but for sheep".[28] Usually Bogle is resigned and patient, and the most bitter comment in the book, with direct application to Galt's own experience, is when a cousin in Jamaica argues that the workers of England suffer greater hardship than the slaves of the West Indies. "You have worse than that—a man may be dragged among you to prison for only a few pounds of debt—is not that slavery?"[29] Even towards emigration, and that is a book intended as a guide for emigrants, Bogle is distinctly unenthusiastic. "Money, the want of it, or to get it, is the actuating spring"[30] . . . "A decision to emigrate for ever . . . is . . . analogous to quitting life."[31]

The last third of the novel (the final chapters of volume two and the whole of volume three) is an account of the settlement of Bogle Corbet in Canada, the part of the book which Galt intended as a guide to emigrants. These Canadian chapters can readily be taken separately to form a book by themselves, as Elizabeth Waterston in fact did for her edition in 1977. "*Bogle Corbet*", she writes in her Introduction, "is the first of a long line of Canadian anti-heroes, given to melancholy, to irony, and to self-mockery. His story offers a wonderfully realistic alternative to the heroic rags-to-riches adventure tales of the American frontier."[32]

Lawrie Todd was such a tale of rags to riches at the frontier of the expanding United States. In *Bogle Corbet* the emphasis is not so much an individual success as on the co-operative development of a community. Bogle, echoing Adam Ferguson, continually stresses "the advantages of reciprocal civility":[33] "if you adhere to each other, your united strength will effect far more with less effort than your utmost separate endeavours. . . . Besides, by beginning with a town you follow the course of Nature, but in scattering yourselves abroad in the forest, you become, as it were, banished men."[34] In urging these arguments to persuade his group of settlers to stay together, Bogle is very conscious of the pull of the United States, to which some of them succumb. There are both economic and political elements in the tension. Bogle recognises "the speculative spirit of the American mind" . . . the economic opportunities of the American system: "In England no just notion prevails of what may be accomplished by the poor man who has only his strength to contribute; but here it is otherwise, and the fair value of a contribution of labour is perfectly understood".[35] Bogle is strongly critical of the British Government's treatment of Canada—"a system indeed so bad, that it might almost justify the supposition that Government, in permitting it to remain unaltered, practised some occult policy to repress the progress of improvement".[36] On the other hand, the political freedom of the United States is seen as one of its great attractions. As one of the settlers remarks, "this gentleman has been telling us that every residenter in the States has the privilege of a hand in the Government, which, considering what we have suffered from the want of that at home, you will allow is a fine thing, and well worthy of a consideration in an o'er sea flitting".[37] Bogle's own decision is, like most of his party, to give the Canadian approach a fair trial. He sees disadvantages in American individualism: "nothing is less disputable than the backwoods-men of the United States have declined from the civilisation of their progenitors".[38]

This Canadian-American tension, involving a conflict between two different views of human society, is so strong an element in the last volume of *Bogle Corbet* that Elisabeth Waterston describes it as "the first major work to define Canadianism by reference to an American alternative".[39] At the same time, no less than *Annals of the Parish*, it is a fable to illustrate an idea of a man as a social animal which is closely akin to Scottish Enlightenment thought. "That is the most happy state . . . and they are most happy men, whose hearts are engaged to a community",[40] wrote Adam Ferguson. The Canadian part of *Bogle Corbet* is an extended demonstration of the same principle.

The Member (Jan 1832); *The Radical* (May 1832)

Towards the end of 1831 Galt was appointed secretary of the British American Land Company and was able to escape from the drudgery of writing three-volume novels to please a publisher, and to write once again to please himself. He produced in quick succession the two political novels, *The Member* and *The Radical*, both imaginary autobiographies and both of a length which suited him, about 30 short chapters. The commissioned novels had appeared with his name; the two new books heralded a return to freedom by attribution to the "Author of The Ayrshire Legatees etc., etc." Both of the books turned on the highly topical question of parliamentary reform, and were indeed later re-issued in one volume under the title, *The Reform*. With so much in common, one might expect them to be very similar. In fact, they are so different in style that it would be impossible to judge on internal evidence alone that they are by the same man.

Part of the difference, but only a part, is that they are aimed at the opposite ends of the political spectrum. As Galt explained in his *Autobiography*: "In the Member, I tried to embody all that could, in my opinion, be urged against the tories of my own way of thinking.... The Radical is more philosophical in the satire; my object in it was to show that many of those institutes, which we regard as essential in society, owe their origin to the sacrifices required to be made by man, to partake of its securities." He says of both books that: "They were undertaken at the time when all the nation were afflicted, not only with the reform mania, but when the public seemed to forget that the first covenant of the social compact, was the surrender of certain natural rights for the privileges and protection of society". Dealing, as they do, with the major political question of the day, the books have all the actuality of journalism. But Galt also says: "Long ago I had meditated to write the Member, so that it was not altogether ephemeral for the time."[41] That may partly explain the difference. *The Member* has many of the characteristics of the *Annals* or *The Provost* and is clearly a product of the same impulse. *The Radical* was probably a quick response to the current political situation. It is more of an extended essay, rather on the 18th-century model, on abstract ideas and a theoretical character type than anything approaching a novel at all. "Very clear but dull", Thackeray commented in his diary, "Written I suppose in a hurry for money."[42]

The narrator of *The Member* is, like Mr Rupees in *The Last of the Lairds*, a Scotsman who has returned home from India "with a decent competency".[43] To meet the financial demands of his numerous relations, he decides that the best investment would be to buy his way into a seat in Parliament where he can use his influence to steer a share of Government patronage in their direction. At first, he has no other political ambitions. He sees no distinction between Whigs and Tories; "a Tory is but a Whig in office, and a Whig but a Tory in opposition, which makes it not difficult for a conscientious man to support the government".[44] But Mr Jobbry is a character who develops. He gradually begins to take a serious interest in the questions of the day. "There is something in the air of the Parliament House that does wile a man on, from day to day, to thole with a great deal of clishmaclavers."[45] He becomes aware of a "change and enlargement" of his mind.[46] The turning point is a meeting with a Mr Selby, a man from the Colonies who, like Galt's own Canadian claimants, had been first promised then repeatedly denied the payment of a legitimate claim for compensation. Mr Jobbry sees that there is a distinction between law and justice[47] (one of Galt's favourite themes), and decides that there was "jarring and jangling in the working of the State".[48] He

develops views on all the issues of the day. Some of these
are surprisingly in advance of their time, such as the
suggestions of an international tribunal to settle disputes
between nations,[49] and of a programme of public works to
reduce unemployment.[50] Mr Jobbry was no die-hard
Tory, but he was opposed to parliamentary reform, or, as
he puts it "giving the unenlightened many, an increase of
dominion over the enlightened few".[51] He sees that his day
is over as the Reform Act looms, and retires to enjoy his
Scottish estate.

There is plenty of irony in *The Member*, but it is directed
more against the system than against Mr Jobbry himself,
even if he remarks that "we are short-sighted creatures and
... self delusion is not uncommon".[52] Indeed Galt tells us
in the *Autobiography* that his model for the character was
quickly identified in the House of Commons but that he
was unlikely to be offended. "I have represented him as
neither saying nor doing aught, that, I think, as the world
wags, he may not unblushingly have done, nor which, in my
heart, I do not approve."[53] Galt does not attribute to Mr
Jobbry the grotesque exaggeration of Indian vocabulary
and allusion of Mr Rupees, who would have been
intolerable as a narrator. Mr Jobbry speaks with the
incisiveness of the shrewd man of affairs. His Scots is much
thinner than Mr Balwhidder's or Provost Pawkie's,
perhaps because this was appropriate for a man who had
spent much of his life in India or perhaps simply because
the book was published in London. His prose, however, is
given flavour and force by the effective use of expressive
Scots words, and there is generally a Scots rhythm to his
sentences. The characters, even the minor ones, are
sharply observed. There is a great deal of comedy,
particularly over the outrageous elections, and the
occasional touch of pathos. The irony is unfaltering:
" 'Trust to Providence, and do your best', cried Mr Tough.
This shows to what desperation our cause was reduced."[54]

The Member, then is unquestionably from the same stable

as the *Annals* and *The Provost* and entirely worthy of being ranked with them. *The Radical* has none of the distinctive qualities of Galt at his best. Even more starkly than *Bogle Corbet*, and in immediate contrast to *The Member*, it shows how much Galt loses when he denies himself his facility in Scots. *The Radical* is written in English in a rotund and abstract style. There is more theorising than narrative, few dialogues and such characters as there are have little life and individuality. There is self-revelation but without much subtlety, some pathos, but no comedy. The interest of the book, for it does have an interest, lies not in the qualities one would expect in a novel, but in its discussion of political ideas.

The narrator, Nathan Butt, is not, as one might expect, a Whig to counterpoise Mr Jobbry, but an extreme Radical. He, too, sees no real difference between Whigs and Tories, but for a different reason. For him the Whigs and Tories only argue about the forms, not the substance. His goal is "nothing less than the emancipation of the human race from the trammels and bondage of the social law".[55] He wants to abolish property, religion, law, marriage and all "coercive expedients in the management of mankind",[56] for "the impulses of nature are justly acknowledged as superior to all artificial maxims and regulations".[57] In practice, he applies the freedom to follow natural impulses only to himself, and expects, for example, absolute obedience from his wife. Like Mr Jobbry he is no democrat, because "the wise are few, and the foolish numerous";[58] but he is prepared to go along with parliamentary reform "as among the means by which my own great and high purposes might be attained".[59] He is elected to Parliament as a Whig but his election was declared invalid because he was found to have been returned "by most flagitious perjury".[60] So he will not be there to vote for the Reform Bill, which was in fact passed in June 1832, only a few weeks after the book was published.

The Radical is really a political pamphlet. Galt deliberately carried the ideas of the Radicals to an anarchistic extreme as a plea for caution towards the dismantling of the complex restraints which society had imposed on natural impulses. Like Walter Scott's, Galt's attitude was consistent with the Scottish Enlightenment view of the complexity of human society and the unpredictable effects of attempts to reform it.[61]

REFERENCES

1. L.L., Vol. I, p. 298.
2. L.L., Vol. I, pp. 296–7.
3. L.L., Vol. I, p. 294.
4. L.T., Pt. I, Chapt. VII.
5. L.T., Pt. VI, Chapt. I.
6. L.L., Vol. I, p. 299.
7. Gordon: p. 93.
8. L.T., Pt. VI, Chapt. II.
9. L.T., Pt. VII, Chapt. III.
10. L.T., Pt. VII, Chapt. VI.
11. L.T., Pt. VIII, Chapt. IX.
12. L.T., Pt. VI, Chapt. II.
13. *Ibid.*
Pt. VI, Chapt. II.
14. *Fraser's Magazine*, Vol. I, March 1830, p. 241.
15. *Chambers's Cyclopaedia of English Literature* (1888), Vol. II, p. 293.
16. L.L., Vol. I, pp. 311–12.
17. Aut., Vol. II, pp. 208–10.
18. Aut., Vol. II, p. 209.
19. As fn. 5 to Chapter I above.
20. Aut., Vol. II, p. 209.
21. *Ibid.*
22. L.L., Vol. I, p. 313.
23. B.C., Vol. I, Chapt. XXXIII, p. 270.
24. B.C., Vol. I, Chapt. XV, p. 118.
25. B.C., Vol. II, Chapt. XVIII, p. 144.
26. B.C., Vol. II, Chaot. XVIII, p. 147.
27. B.C., Vol. II, Chapt. XVII, p. 142.
28. B.C., Vol. II, Chapt. XIX, p. 220.

29. B.C., Vol. II, Chapt. IV, p. 26.
30. B.C., Vol. II, Chapt. XXX, p. 233.
31. B.C., Vol. II, Chapt. XXII, p. 182.
32. Elizabeth Waterston; edition of *Bogle Corbet* (Vol. III)—(1977) Introduction p. i.
33. B.C., Vol. III (1977 ed.), Chapt. XXX, p. 120.
34. B.C., Vol. III (1977 ed.), Chapt. XV, p. 66.
35. B.C., Vol. III (1977 ed.), Chapt. XLIII, pp. 172–3.
36. B.C., Vol. III (1977 ed.), Chapt. XXIX, p. 118.
37. B.C., Vol. III (1977 ed.), Chapt. XIII, p. 59.
38. B.C., Vol. II (1977 ed.), Chapt. XXIX, p. 118.
39. As 32 above, p. 2.
40. Ferguson, p. 58.
41. Aut. Vol. II, pp. 250–1.
42. *The Letters and Private Papers of W. M. Thackeray*, ed. Gordon N. Ray (1945), Vol. I, p. 201.
43. Mem., Chapt. I, p. 3.
44. Mem., Chapt. II, p. 7.
45. Mem., Chapt. XXVI, p. 87.
46. Mem., Chapt. XXXII, p. 105.
47. Mem., Chapt. XVIII, p. 61.
48. Mem., Chapt. XIX, p. 64.
49. Mem., Chapt. XXIX, p. 96.
50. Mem., Chapt. XXXV, p. 117.
51. Mem., Chapt. XIX, p. 66.
52. Mem., Chapt. VII, p. 24.
53. Aut., Vol. II, p. 251.
54. Mem., Chapt. XXI, p. 73.
55. Rad., Chapt. XVII, p. 132.
56. Rad., Chapt. II, p. 16.
57. Rad., Chapt. VI, p. 55.
58. Rad., Chapt. XIX, p. 148.
59. Rad., Chapt. XVII, p. 132.
60. Rad., Conclusion, p. 199.
61. See on this point my paper in *Scott and his Influence* (as fn. 10 to Chapt. I).

CHAPTER X

THE CRITICAL RESPONSE

In the last 150 years, Galt's critical reputation has not been constant. It stood very high in his own lifetime, when he was admired by Scott, Byron and Coleridge and most of the critical reviews of the time. There was then a period of decline, although he continued to be published and presumably, therefore, read. The first revival came about 1896, when Blackwood's published a collected, but far from complete, edition of several of the novels and a notable essay. A second revival in the 1930s coincided, or was stimulated by, another similar edition (but this time including *Ringan Gilhaize*) published by John Grant of Edinburgh in 1936. Since then, Galt has been subject to a more detailed and penetrating analysis by American, Swedish and French, as well as Scottish, critics and literary historians. With some dissident voices, this has now established his reputation on deeper and more secure foundations than at any time in the past.

Galt's earliest critics were quick to recognize many of his distinctive strengths, the accuracy of his observation, the verisimilitude of his narrative, especially in his imaginary autobiographies, his skill in the creation and analysis of character, his handling of both the comic and the pathetic, his irony, his social and political awareness, and his linguistic dexterity in Scots. The doyen of Scottish letters, Henry Mackenzie, although not normally a contributor to *Blackwood's Magazine*, wrote for them an appreciation of the *Annals of the Parish*. This appeared in the issue of May 1821, immediately after the publication of the book. The *Annals*, he said:

place before us the figures as they are seen in every village with which we are acquainted . . . we see them at their doors or their firesides. They look, and speak, and act, as is natural to their situation; . . . the pathetic is that of ordinary, not high-wrought feeling, and its language the natural expression of affliction without the swell of tragedy, or the whine of sentiment.

The early absolution of Galt from the charge of sentimentality is especially interesting in coming, as it does, from the pen of the author of *The Man of Feeling* himself.

The *Literary Gazette* suggested that Galt was the literary equivalent to the Flemish masters in painting and spoke of his "delightful union of the humorous and pathetic".[1] On another occasion, they said that they were tempted to believe that Galt was in possession of some magic spell, "so actual, so individual are the characters he sketches, or rather creates. He possesses, in a most eminent degree, that peculiar talent which, to this day, makes Robinson Crusoe a thing of tangible memory and actual existence."[2] *Fraser's Magazine* in reviewing *The Member* found "caustic sagacity" on every page, and an irony "so exquisite, as to mislead even the most discerning".[3] *The Spectator* considered, "As a fictitious autobiographer Mr Galt surpasses every writer, certainly of this day, perhaps of any time".[4]

Of these early notices, probably the most influential was the one which Francis Jeffrey wrote for the *Edinburgh Review* of October 1823. This dealt with all the "Tales of the West" up to *The Entail* as well as *Ringan Gilhaize* and with some novels of Lockhart and John Wilson. The title of Jeffrey's essay was "Secondary Scotch Novels", but this was not intended to be derogatory. By "secondary" he meant in relation to Sir Walter Scott, then accepted by everyone as the supreme master of the novel. And it was an age, as Ian Jack remarks in the *Oxford History of English Literature*, when "a number of the ablest writers of prose fiction at this time were Scots, notably John Galt, Susan Ferrier, Lockhart and James Hogg".[5] Although he damned *The Steamboat* and *Ringan Gilhaize*, the general tone of Jeffrey's review was highly favourable to Galt. He spoke of his "traits of shy and sarcastic sagacity, and occasionally softened and relieved by touches of unexpected tenderness and simple pathos, all harmonised by the same truth to nature and fine sense of national peculiarity". In two respects, Jeffrey even found Galt superior to Scott: "There is also more systematic, though very good-humoured, sarcasm, and a more distinct moral, or unity of didactic purpose, in most of his writings, than it would be easy to discover in the playful, capricious, and fanciful sketches of his great master."[6]

Jeffrey was not alone in recognising the serious underlying purposes of Galt's novels. John Wilson in a "Letter from an Occasional Contributor" to *Blackwood's Magazine* of June 1822 said of *The Provost*: "There is far more truth and nature, and moral philosophy, and metaphysics, and politics, and political economy in this little volume, than in all Dugald Stewart and the *Scotsman*". *Fraser's Magazine* said of *The Member* that the narrator "with smiling humour, but profound prudence, observes more or less upon every important question that has recently agitated the councils of the nation", and that the book was full of "deep sagacity and of the highest political import".[7] Similarly, the *Literary Gazette* said of *Lawrie Todd* that it contained "a treatise on political economy".[8]

There was, however, unhappily for Galt's reputation, another respect in which Jeffrey's review reflected, or provoked, a reaction to the novels which began to assert itself. Several times, Jeffrey accused Galt of vulgarity. Even *The Ayrshire Legatees* had "too much vulgarity"; *The Steamboat* was a "series of vulgar stories"; *The Entail* was marked by a "tone of wilful vulgarity". Similarly, the *Quarterly Review*, while it was "pleased and affected by the Chronicle of Dalmailing", thought that "some of the expressions put into the mouth of Mr Cayenne . . . are of a brutal and shocking impiety . . . which no gentleman could have uttered and which no Christian minister should have recorded".[9] Of *Lawrie Todd, Frazer's Magazine* said: "There is not another author of the present day, perhaps, but Mr Galt would have ventured to break through the starched manner of our time with such a scene as that with Miss Beeny Needles".[10] In one of John Wilson's imaginary dialogues in *Blackwood's Magazine*, the *Noctes Ambrosianae*, Christopher North (Wilson himself) and the shepherd (James Hogg) discuss Galt:

> North: "Mr Galt is a man of genius. . . . His humour is rich, rare and racy. . . . He is conversant, not only with many modes and manners of life, but with much of its hidden and mysterious spirit."
>
> Shepherd: "He's aften unco coorse."
>
> North: "True, James, he is not so uniformly delicate and refined as you are in your prose compositions."[11]

In Chapter VII, I discussed the way in which this accusation of vulgarity bedevilled his relationship with William Blackwood over the manuscript of *The Last of the Lairds*. In his brilliant biography of Galt, Ian Gordon has described how Galt was cold-shouldered by the sons who took over the firm as soon as William Blackwood himself died in 1834.[12] Only a year or two before, Galt's critical standing had seemed safe, with the almost unanimous praise for his "Tales of the West" from the literary reviews. There was a sudden collapse. R. P. Gillies, who knew Galt personally, was very soon writing in these terms in his *Memoirs of a Literary Veteran* (published in 1851): "I suspect such productions would not tell equally now-a-days, but at that time, his 'Ayrshire Legatees' and other works of the same class were very popular".[13] Mrs Margaret Oliphant, herself a Blackwood's author, reflected the new disapproval of Galt by damning him with faint praise when she wrote the history of the firm in 1847. Galt, she wrote, was "one whose great temporary reputation, very real while it lasted, fell for a time into oblivion,—but is, we hope, rising again into a modest revival".[14]

How is this sudden descent of Galt from critical esteem to oblivion to be explained? There is, of course, a fashion in these matters and many writers of established reputation go through a period of neglect after their death. In Galt's case, the transition came so rapidly and abruptly that it needs some other explanation. It was not because his reputation had been damaged by his later novels. Some were dull enough, but *Lawrie Todd* and *The Member* were highly praised. I suspect that the truth is that Galt was a victim of the increasing gentility, "starched manner", and evangelical religiosity of the age. It is noticeable that the passages which are singled out for adverse comment are invariably those which might offend religious sensibility (like Mr Cayenne) or sexual prudery (like Beeny Needles).

I do not think that it was the fact that Galt used Scots, as opposed to standard English, which provoked the charge of vulgarity or the withdrawal of critical approval. This was, after all, the age when Sir Walter Scott was at the height of both popular and critical success and had made Scots dialogue acceptable, even in England. Galt, in fact, in *Bogle Corbet* refers to "the fashion to consider Scotch as a classical language and worthy of acquiring, to enable all the world to understand the words of the Border Minstrel".[15] Jeffrey himself, as Carlyle tells us, had Scots "in store, in excellent condition, to the very end of his life",[16] and in his Essay on Burns had made an eloquent defence of its literary value: "not to be considered as a provincial dialect ... the language of a great body of poetry ... a highly poetical language".[17] Galt's own use of Scots earned nothing but praise, even if John Wilson Croker complained privately to Blackwood that he could not understand it.[18] Margaret Oliphant, for instance, said that: "It was usually (except when a peasant of the lowest order was speaking) fine old-fashioned Scotch, the Scotch of the old ministers and the old ladies, full of idioms and curious constructions, not dialect at all".[29] S. R. Crockett made a similar point: "When Galt writes in Scots, he writes the language and not the dialect belonging to any particular locality. He is in the main stream. He belongs to the great tradition."[20]

No doubt, Galt's Scots did become something of an obstacle to appreciation of his work in certain circles and in certain places, but at a later period, when the Waverley enthusiasm waned. V. S. Pritchett, writing in 1946, and speaking of England said: "At some time in the last 30 years feeling against dialect and especially the Scottish dialect had hardened into a final dislike".[21] He may have been right for a time, but I suspect that in this, as in other matters of taste, there is no finality. It is also true, as the American Harvey Oxenhorn said of MacDiarmid, that those who allow Scots to comprise an obstacle betray their own "provinciality and lethargy".[22] It is possible that the long-term effects of MacDiarmid's poetry and of Lorimer's translation of the *New Testament* may restore Scots to favour as a literary language.

An aspect of the genteel disapproval of Galt was the belief that he presented an untrue and unflattering picture of the Scottish character. As we have seen, this was the view of the novelist, Jane Findlater (1866–1946). "There is no doubt", she wrote, "that Galt's novels have gone far to establish the unpleasant popular idea of the Scottish character. He is very unfair to his countrymen: all his vital characters—those that make his books—are singularly unlovely. Those that are meant to be good are very vulgar: those that are bad are not credited with one redeeming quality. . . . Greed, coarseness, meanness are his constant themes. . . . His men are all misers."[23] Again, the key words, vulgar and coarse. A similar view is expressed in an undated pamphlet of about the turn of the century by James Leatham, *John Galt, the First of the Kailyarders; A Neglected Man of Genius and Why.*[26] This argues that Galt "has had his day" and deserves obscurity, precisely because he gave the sort of picture of the Scots of which Jane Findlater complained. This is a late 19th-century view of the matter. It comes from a generation reared on the pious evasions of the Kailyard who cannot stomach Galt, because he is not a Kailyarder and does not flinch from reality. All that Galt has in common with the Kailyard is the setting and the language. In intellectual attitude, in realism and honesty, he is poles apart.

The critical neglect of Galt in the mid-19th century did not prevent the constant reprinting of most of the "Tales of the West". He evidently still found readers, even if the critics ignored him. In the 19th century, there were at least nine editions of the *Annals of the Parish*, eight of *The Ayrshire Legatees*, and *The Entail* and *Sir Andrew Wylie*, six of *The Provost* and three of *The Last of the Lairds*. It is true, as Ian Gordon points out,[23] that all of these were titles originally published by Blackwood's, which they continued to promote and keep in print in the Standard Novels series. The "Collected Edition" which Blackwood's published in 1895 and 1896 included these books and no others. Other books, including *Ringan Gilhaize, Lawrie Todd, Bogle Corbet* and *The Member*, as well as the short stories, tended to be ignored, simply because they did not have a publisher with the staying power of Blackwood's behind them. *Ringan Gilhaize* was not reprinted after its first edition of 1823 until 1870. *The Member* was not reprinted, apart from its reissue along with *The Radical* in 1833, until Ian Gordon himself edited his edition in 1975. On the other hand, Gordon's point does not apply to *Lawrie Todd*, which had four British and sixteen American editions.[26]

Incomplete as it was, the Blackwood's Collected Edition of 1895/6, edited by D. Storrar Meldrum with Introduction by S. R. Crockett, seems to have given the stimulus to the revival of critical interest in Galt. It was closely followed by the first book substantially devoted to Galt and his work, Sir George Douglas's *The Blackwood Group*, published in the "Famous Scots" series in 1897. This was mainly notable for its advocacy of *Ringan Gilhaize* as "a neglected masterpiece", as he described it in the edition which he edited in the following year. Perhaps even more significant was an essay, published in *Blackwood's Magazine* of June 1896, by J. H. Millar as a review of the Collected Edition.[27] In this, the future author of *A Literary History of Scotland* made a number of important points. He saw that Galt was closely connected with the Scottish Enlightenment, or as he called it "the Scots Renaissance in the second half of the 18th century"; and that he "noted, with an observation that amounts to philosophic insight, the developmental forces beneath contemporary events". Galt's Dalmailing and Gudetown were "the nation in miniature. And to achieve dramatic history in this way, embodying the general in the particular is, perhaps, what has been done by no one else." Millar made a sharp distinction between Galt and the Kailyard or the school which had been written by and for a religious public. That school was "a triple lie ... deceiving the writer and deceiving the reader and a libel on life itself". Galt, on the contrary, saw life whole and complete. In other words, Millar, in direct reaction to the school of writing which evolved from the cult of gentility, saw virtue in Galt's so-called vulgarity and coarseness. Galt was, at last, emerging from the odium of prim disapproval which had clung to him from the time of Francis Jeffrey's essay.

It is curious that Millar's review, which is very remarkable for the time when it was written, does not seem to have been much commented upon by subsequent critics of Galt.[28] Whether they are conscious of it or not, the fact is that much of the new critical interest in Galt amounts to extended examinations of the propositions advanced by J. H. Millar in 1896.

Ironically, the Introductions to the Collected Edition by S. R. Crockett reflect an utterly different attitude, as one might expect from one of the delvers in the Kailyard.

Crocket is an enthusiast for Galt. Indeed he claims the
credit for putting the idea of a Collected Edition in the
mind of the publisher by a chance remark "expressing
admiration and appreciation of Galt". But he admires
Galt for very different reasons from J. H. Millar's. Crockett
sees that Galt has a "vivid directness and reality" and an
"exquisite fidelity, in which the art is so concealed that
we can hardly believe in its existence". For Crockett,
however, this technique is applied to the description of a
peaceful country life, in which nothing happens. "There
are no books in our national literature which convey so
melodious and continuous an impression of peace." They
have a "restfulness like a Scottish Sabbath day in the older
times". For Crockett, all the irony, all the concern with
social and political change, all the underlying themes are
evidently invisible. He did not, like Millar, see the general
in the particular. His conclusion must be the most
damning praise ever inflicted on a writer: "I do not
mistake Galt for either a great writer or a great man. . . .
He is like the best oatmeal porridge—with cream."[24] This
very limited view of Galt did not die readily. In fact, one
could say that subsequent Galt criticism resolves itself into
the Millar and Crockett schools.

Galt's critical reputation continued to establish itself in
the early decades of the present century, recognised by the
inclusion of the *Annals of the Parish*, *The Ayrshire Legatees*
and *The Entail* in such series as Everyman's Library, World
Classics and Nelson's Classics. The first full-length book
devoted exclusively to his life and work, *John Galt* by R. K.
Gordon, was published in Toronto in 1920. A. J. Ashley,
who communicated Coleridge's marginal note on *The
Provost* in a letter of 25 September 1930 to the *Times Literary
Supplement*, referred to the "steadily growing popularity of
Galt's novels". Once again, a surge of interest was
stimulated by, or at least coincided with, the publication of
a Collected Edition. This was the set limited to the usual
titles, but with the addition of *Ringan Gilhaize*, published by

John Grant of Edinburgh in 1936 and edited by D. S. Meldrum and William Roughead. The Bibliography by H. Lumsden and the biography by J. W. Aberdein appeared in the same year.

The publication of the biography and the new Collected Edition was noticed in a long article in the *Times Literary Supplement* of 31 October 1936, "Dominion and Parish: John Galt's Conquest of Two Worlds", which was anonymous, but almost certainly written by Agnes Mure Mackenzie. Like Millar forty years earlier, this saw Galt as belonging to "that brilliant Scots Risorgimento", or, in other words, to the Scottish Enlightenment. It described him as "the father of the modern novel of analysis", with "keen moral judgement and pity" and "a rich sense of absurdity". Of the *Annals of the Parish* and *The Provost*, it said this:

> Both are aesthetically near perfection, with the union of broad design and delicate finish of realistic detail that one has in Dutch painting, although their temper is closer to French than Dutch. *The Provost* indeed anticipates Balzac . . . or recalls Molière. It is, superbly, that projection of the universal through the particular that is one of the definitions of art.[36]

F. H. Lyell's *A Study of the Novels of John Galt* published in Princeton in 1942, although more descriptive than critical, was the first detailed account of the whole range of Galt's work. A similar, comprehensive survey was undertaken by another American in 1978, Ruth Aldrich in her *John Galt* (Boston). Erik Frykman in his *John Galt's Scottish Stories 1820–1823* (Uppsala 1959) subjected that part of Galt's work to a more rigorous analysis and tended to reject some of the larger claims that have been made for him. Both in this book, and more particularly in a lecture to the Greenock Philosophical Society,[31] Frykman was the first critic to draw attention to the influence on Galt of the works of the Scottish Enlightenment which were available to him in the Greenock Subscription Library. This aspect has since been studied in more detail by K. M. Costain and others.[32]

The gradual revival of Galt's critical reputation and of the Millar view can be traced in the standard histories of literature. In 1915, the *Cambridge History of English Literature* gave only nine lines to Galt, which were complimentary enough but entirely superficial. By 1935, Ernest Baker, in *The History of the English Novel*, gave him several pages and saw "reflections that would not discredit a sociologist having more than average insight into human nature".[33] Walter Allen in *The English Novel*, first published in 1954, wrote: "There is . . . a robust grasp of the facts of everyday reality and a raciness in the rendering of it. . . . He was anything but a provincial writer. A novel like *The Entail* has in many ways much closer affinity with the work of Gogol or even Dostoyevsky in some of his phases than with the great majority of his English contemporaries."[34] Kurt Witting in *The Scottish Tradition in Literature* in 1958: "John Galt's sensitive awareness of *contemporary* social and economic changes was a new gift to Scottish literature, and his insight into contemporary Scottish life went much deeper even than Fergusson's".[25] In 1963, Ian Jack in Vol. X of the *Oxford History of English Literature* gave the best part of a chapter to Galt. He spoke of his "rare gifts" and added: "Galt was a born sociologist . . . an exceptionally perceptive observer of the changes in the pattern of society which were going on in the Lowlands of Scotland in his day".[36]

The counter-attack on the Millar view came from an unlikely quarter. At first sight, there is very little in common between S. R. Crockett and David Craig, the Marxist critic and the author of *Scottish Literature and the Scottish People* (1961), but both have in common a refusal to see anything in Galt's novels beneath the obvious surface appearance. The essential difference between them in this respect is that Crockett admired and enjoyed what he saw on the surface; Craig profoundly disliked it. "Galt", he considers, "has no motive beyond the imitation of the immediately available surface life." Of Mr Balwhidder, he says: "Because the minister is as conservative and credulous as many of his parishioners, and because everything is felt through his mentality, all other possible life is diminished to his kind of understanding". Generally, "Galt's very medium—the imitation of local speech and outlook—is bound to immerse him in . . . parochialism".[37] This condescension towards the language which the great majority actually spoke is a curious attitude for a professed Marxist.

"Parochial" is one of these sweeping terms of abuse which is rarely defined or understood. What does it mean in relation to Galt? Let us leave aside, for the moment, the books in which Galt ranged over the Mediterranean and North America and consider only the *Annals* and *The Provost*, which are firmly set within a parish or two in, and close to, Irvine. They are parochial in the literal sense, very precisely in the case of the *Annals*, that they deal with events in one parish. On the other hand, they both show greater awareness of what is going on in the rest of the world, the French Revolution, the American War and so on, than, say, the novels of Jane Austen. Secondly, in the opinion of contemporaries such as Henry Mackenzie, Galt's accounts of Dalmailing and Gudetown were applicable to the whole of Lowland Scotland. Then, and perhaps this is the most important point, even if David Craig does not agree, Galt's themes, the nature of social and economic change in the *Annals* and of political power in *The Provost*, have a universal application. Is Galt then 'parochial' in any meaningful sense?

David Craig attributes Galt's attitudes, or his parochialism as he would have it, to *Blackwood's Magazine*. Galt, he says, "headed a squad of writings, centred on Blackwood's publishing house and *Blackwood's Magazine* which set out to publish writing in Scots and to 'do' provincial Scotland".[38]

In fact, Galt was never a member of the Blackwood's inner circle, far less its leader, in the way that Lockhart, Hogg and Wilson were. He was very much his own man and more often in conflict with William Blackwood than in agreement.

The American scholar, Francis Hart, takes up this question in his important book, *The Scottish Novel* (1978). He thinks that David Craig was right to see Galt in the context of Blackwood's, but he disagrees with Craig's view that this milieu was, at that time at least, "reactionary" or "provincial". He goes to describe the Blackwood circle in these terms: "Its nationalism was sometimes authentic, its romanticism Germanic or Coleridgian, its radical Toryism the immediate ancestor of the Fraserians and Thomas Carlyle. Blackwoodian reaction is the manifestation of a Scottish counter-enlightenment."[39] Whether or not this is true of the Blackwoodians as a whole, and that is a subject in itself, it certainly hardly applies to Galt. His nationalism was authentic, but in every other respect Galt does not fit into any of Hart's categories. Galt was no romantic, and he failed whenever he tried to act the part, either to please William Blackwood or for any other reason. He was not so much a radical Tory, as an instinctive Radical who masqueraded as a Tory. He did not react against the Scottish Enlightenment, but adopted its essential principles and sought to illustrate them by other means. It seems to me, therefore, that the attempt of Craig and Hart to consider Galt in a purely Blackwoodian context has been more misleading than helpful. This is a cul-de-sac in the main road of criticism which has developed since Millar's essay in 1896.

No one has done more in this century to extend an awareness and understanding of Galt than Ian Gordon. His admirable biography, *John Galt: The Life of a Writer*, was published in 1972. It not only brought Galt to life as a man, but made many judicious comments on the whole range of his work. His editions have restored *The Member*, several of the short stories and Galt's original version of *The Last of the Lairds* to circulation, and his notes on *The Provost* and *The Entail* have thrown new light on them.

Nineteen seventy-nine, the bicentenary of Galt's birth, produced two important books, a collection of perceptive essays, *John Galt 1779–1979*, edited by G. A. Whatley, and a comprehensive study of the novels, *John Galt: Romancier Ecossais* by Henri Gibault. He sums up Galt's Scottish novels in these words: "La civilisation y est surprise dans le mouvement des forces historiques qui l'entraînent; on y percoit la synthèse organique de l'individu et de son époque, avec autant de netteté que chez Scott et chez Balzac", and he concludes "Ce dont Galt a besoin c'est d'une réévaluation patiente, d'une investigation dans tout les secteurs négligés de son ouvre immense, menée parallèlement a une réédition critique qui ne se limiterait pas aux ouvres periodiquement republiées. Galt prendra alors se véritable dimension de romancier dont on a sous-estime l'originalité et l'envergure. Ces travaux en vue d'une appréciation globale ne font que commencer."[40] To this re-evaluation, Henri Gibault himself has already made a distinguished contribution.

In his *History of Scottish Literature* (1977), Maurice Lindsay said: "By and large, Galt's novels remain essentially a Scottish taste, for the same reason as do the poems of Fergusson. Both are inherently so affectionately involved with the nuances of the Scots tongue that much of their best work is not only untranslatable, but is only of limited interest to that outside majority of readers who have scant patience with what they are pleased to regard as 'dialect' writing."[41] Others have made a similar point. J. H. Millar in his *A Literary History of Scotland* (1903) said that "no one not a Scot can adequately appreciate the delicacy of Galt's strokes",[42] and in his *Blackwood's* essay remarked that the Scottish reader of Galt was "constantly surprised into a delighted recognition".[43] Jeffrey said much the same of Burns:

. . . we must take leave to apprise our Southern readers, that all his best pieces are written in Scotch; and that it is impossible for them to form any adequate judgment of their merits, without a pretty long residence among those who still use that language. To be able to translate the words, is but a small part of the knowledge that is necessary. The whole genius and idiom of the language must be familiar; and the characters, and habits, and associations of those who speak it.[44]

There is, no doubt, an element of truth in these remarks. At the same time, perhaps they underestimate the extent to which a non-Scottish reader, with a little effort, can share the pleasure. The international reputation of Burns suggests that this is so. With his fellow Ayrshireman, John Galt, a striking fact is that of the nine books about him published in this century, two have been published in Canada, two in the United States, one in Sweden and one in France. Perhaps that is as good an indication of any of the universality of his appeal.

REFERENCES

1. *Literary Gazette*, No. 283, 22 June 1822, pp. 386–7.
2. *Literary Gazette*, No. 680, 30 January 1830, p. 67.
3. *Fraser's Magazine*, Vol. V, April 1832, pp. 369 & 371.
4. *The Spectator*, Vol. IV, 14 May 1831, p. 474.
5. Ian Jack, *op. cit.*, Vol. X, p. 226.
6. Jeffrey, Vol. III, pp. 499 & 500.
7. *Fraser's Magazine*, Vol. V, April 1832, pp. 374 & 371.
8. *Literary Gazette*, No. 680, 30 January 1830, p. 68.
9. *Quarterly Review*, Vol. XXV, April 1821, p. 153.
10. *Fraser's Magazine*, Vol. I, March 1830, p. 241.
11. "Noctes Ambrosianae", No. LII in *Blackwood's Magazine*, Vol. XXVIII, November 1830, p. 843.
12. Gordon, pp. 122–3.

13. R. P. Gillies, *op. cit.*, Vol. III, p. 57.
14. Oliphant, Vol. I, p. 45.
15. B.C., Chapt. IV.
16. Thomas Carlyle, *Reminiscences* (Everyman's Library edition, 1972), p. 334.
17. Jeffrey, Vol. II, pp. 401–2.
18. Oliphant, Vol. I, p. 449.
19. Oliphant, Vol. I, p. 450.
20. S. R. Crockett, Introduction to *Annals of the Parish* (1895), p. xli.
21. V. S. Pritchett, *The Living Novel* (1946), p. 43.
22. Harvey Oxenhorn, *Elemental Things: The Poetry of Hugh MacDiarmid* (1984), p. 192.
23. Jane Helen Findlater, *Stones From a Glass House* (1904), pp. 95–6.
24. James Leatham, *op cit.* (ND), p. 8.
25. Gordon, p. 143.
26. H. Lumsden, *Bibliography of John Galt; Records of Glasgow Bibliographical Society*, Vol. IX (1931); and Aldrich, *op. cit.*, p. 127 for American editions of *Lawrie Todd*.
27. *Blackwood's Magazine*, Vol. CLIX.
28. It is, however, mentioned in a footnote by K. M. Costain in his paper, "The Prince and the Provost" (see fn. 6 to Chapter V above).
29. S. R. Crockett, *op. cit.*, pp. xvii, xxxiv, xxxvi, xxxvii, xiv.
30. I am indebted to Willis Pickard for the information that the *TLS* archives record only that the article was written by Miss Mackenzie. From the style, there is little doubt that this was Agnes Mure Mackenzie.
31. Erik Frykman, "John Galt and 18th Century Scottish Philosophy". The John Galt Lecture for 1953. *Papers of the Greenock Philosophical Society* (1954).
32. Keith M. Costain, Theoretical History and the Novel: The Scottish Fiction of John Galt. *English Literary History*, Vol. 43, n. 3 (Fall 1976), pp. 342–65.
33. Ernest A. Baker, *The History of the English Novel* (1935), Vol. VI, p. 235.
34. Walter Allen, *The English Novel* (1954), Pelican Edition (1973), pp. 127 & 129.
35. Kurt Wittig, *The Scottish Tradition in Literature* (1958), p. 252.
36. Jan Jack, *Oxford History of English Literature*, Vol. X (1815-1832), (1963), pp. 229 & 235.
37. David Craig, *Scottish Literature and the Scottish People: 1680–1830* (1961), pp. 157, 158 & 159.
38. *Ibid.*, p. 157.
39. Francis Russell Hart, *The Scottish Novel* (1978), p. 31.
40. Henri Gibault, *John Galt: Romancier Ecossais* (1979), pp. 220–1 & 221–2.

41. Maurice Lindsay, *History of Scottish Literature* (1977), p. 320.
42. J. H. Millar, *A Literary History of Scotland* (1903), p. 554.
43. J. H. Millar, "The Novels of John Galt", in *Blackwood's Magazine*, Vol. CLIX, June 1896, p. 871.
44. Jeffrey, Vol. II, p. 401.

SELECT BIBLIOGRAPHY

H. Lumsden's *Bibliography of John Galt* (Records of Glasgow Bibliographical Society, Vol. IX, 1931) lists most of the British, but few of the American, editions up to that date. It does not help with the critical and biographical works about Galt, because most of these have been published since then. There are useful bibliographies in the books by Frykman, Lyell and Ian Gordon.

Ian Gordon's *John Galt: The Life of a Writer* supersedes all previous biographies and the collection of essays edited by C. A. Whatley, *John Galt: 1779–1979*, is an excellent résumé of contemporary scholarship.

I. PRINCIPAL WORKS OF JOHN GALT

Biographical Sketch of John Wilson (in *Scotish* (sic) *Descriptive Poems*, edited by John Leyden)	1803
Life of Cardinal Wolsey: Tragedies, Voyages and Travels 1809–1811	1812
Letters from the Levant	1813
The New British Theatre (editor and contributor)	1814
The Majolo: A Tale—Life of Benjamin West	1816
Glenfell or MacDonalds and Campbells	1820
The Ayrshire Legatees—The Earthquake	1820
The Steamboat—Annals of the Parish	1821
Sir Andrew Wylie—The Provost—The Gathering of the West— The Entail	1822
Ringan Gilhaize—The Spae Wife	1823
Rothelan	1824
The Omen	1825
The Last of the Lairds	1826
Lawrie Todd—Southennan—Life of Lord Byron	1830
Bogle Corbet	1831
The Member—The Radical	1832
Eben Erskine—Poems—Autobiography	1833
Literary Life and Miscellanies	1834

II. COLLECTED (BUT FAR FROM COMPLETE) EDITIONS

The Works of John Galt, edited by D. Storrar Meldrum
with Introduction by S. R. Crockett (Blackwood's,
Edinburgh)   1895–96
(Includes: *Annals of the Parish, Ayrshire Legatees, Sir
Andrew Wylie, The Entail, The Provost, The Last of the
Lairds*)

The Works of John Galt, edited by D. S. Meldrum and
William Roughead (John Grant, Edinburgh)   1936
(Adds *Ringan Gilhaize*)

III. RECENT EDITIONS

Annals of the Parish, edited by James Kinsley (Oxford
English Novels)   1967
The Entail, edited by Ian A. Gordon (Oxford English
Novels)   1970
—Reprinted in "World's Classics" series (paperback)   1984
The Provost, edited by Ian A. Gordon (Oxford English
Novels)   1973
—Reprinted in "World's Classics" series (paperback)   1982
The Member, edited by Ian A. Gordon (Scottish Academic
Press for the Association for Scottish Literary Studies)   1975
The Last of the Lairds, edited by Ian A. Gordon (Scottish
Academic Press)   1976
Bogle Corbet, (Vol. III with a few chapters of Vol. II),
edited by Elizabeth Waterston (New Canadian
Library)   1977
The Ayrshire Legatees (Mercat Press, Edinburgh)   1978
Selected Short Stories, edited by Ian A. Gordon (Scottish
Academic Press for A.S.L.S.)   1978
Annals of the Parish (Mercat Press, Edinburgh)   1980
Ringan Gilhaize, edited by Patricia J. Wilson (Scottish
Academic Press for A.S.L.S.)   forthcoming

IV. BOOKS ABOUT (OR PARTLY ABOUT) GALT

Margaret Oliphant, *Annals of a Publishing House: William
Blackwood and Sons* (Edinburgh)   1847
Sir George Douglas, *The Blackwood Group* (Famous Scots
Series) (Edinburgh)   1897

R. K. Gordon, *John Galt* (Toronto)   1920

Jennie W. Aberdein, *John Galt* (Oxford)   1936

F. H. Lyell, *A Study of the Novels of John Galt* (Princeton)   1942

Erik Frykman, *John Galt's Scottish Stories 1820–1823* (Uppsala)   1959

David Craig, *Scottish Literature and the Scottish People: 1680–1830* (London)   1961

W. W. Parker, *Susan Ferrier and John Galt* (London)   1965

Ian A. Gordon, *John Galt: The Life of a Writer* (Edinburgh)   1972

Ruth Aldrich, *John Galt* (Boston)   1978

Francis Russell Hart, *The Scottish Novel: A Critical Survey* (London)   1978

Christopher A. Whatley (Ed.), *John Galt 1779–1979* (Edinburgh)   1979

(Contains essays by Ian A. Gordon, Annand C. Chitnis, Christopher A. Whatley, Kenneth G. Simpson, Ian Campbell, John MacQueen, Patricia J. Wilson, John T. Ward, Keith Costain and J. Derrick McClure)

Henri Gibault, *John Galt: Romancier Ecossais* (Grenoble)   1979

Scottish Literary Journal, John Galt Number (Vol. 8, N.I.)   May 1981

(Contains essays by Ian A. Gordon, Keith Costain, J. D. McClure and Patricia J. Wilson)

V. REVIEWS AND CRITICAL ESSAYS

Henry Mackenzie, Review of *Annals of the Parish*— *Blackwood's Magazine*, Vol. IX   May 1821

John Wilson (Christopher North), "Letter of Thanks from an Occasional Contributor", *Blackwood's Magazine*, Vol. XI   June 1822

Francis Jeffrey, "Secondary Scotch Novels", *Edinburgh Review*, in *Contributions to the Edinburgh Review*, Vol. III (London, 1844)   Oct. 1823

John Wilson, "Noctes Ambrosianae", No. LII, *Blackwood's Magazine*, Vol. XXVIII   Nov. 1830

J. H. Millar, "The Novels of John Galt", *Blackwood's Magazine*, Vol. CLIX   Jun. 1896

George Kitchin: "John Galt" in *Edinburgh Essays on Scots Literature* (Edinburgh) — 1933

Agnes Mure Mackenzie (probable attribution), "Dominion and Parish: John Galt's Conquest of Two Worlds"—*Times Literary Supplement* — 31 Oct. 1936

The Papers of the Greenock Philosophical Society

  James Bridie, "The Scottish Character as it was viewed from Galt to Barrie" — 1937

  Thomas W. Hamilton, "John Galt: The Man, his Life and Work" — 1946

  Douglas Young, "The Use of Scots for Prose" — 1949

  William Brownlie, "John Galt: Social Historian" — 1951

  Erik Frykman, "John Galt and 18th Century Scottish Philosophy" — 1953

  W. Croft Dickinson: "John Galt; *The Provost* and the Burgh" — 1954

John MacQueen, "John Galt and the Analysis of Social History" in *Scott Bicentenary Essays*, ed. Alan Bell (Edinburgh) — 1973

Charles Swann, "Past into Present: Scott, Galt and the Historical Novel" in *Literature and History*, No. 3 — March 1976

Keith Costain, "The Prince and The Provost" in *Studies in English Literature*, Vol. VI, No. 1 — 1968

Keith Costain, "Theoretical History and the Novel: The Scottish Fiction of John Galt" in *English Literary History*, Vol. 43, No. 3 — Fall 1976

Keith Costain, "The Spirit of the Age and the Scottish Fiction of John Galt" in *The Wordsworth Circle* — Spring 1980

Alan MacGillivray: "Galt in the Schools" in *Scottish Literary Journal* (Supplement No. 13) — Winter 1980